CHRISTIAN SPIRITUALITY AND
SACRAMENTAL COMMUNITY

Christian Spirituality and Sacramental Community

WOLFHART PANNENBERG

Darton, Longman and Todd
London

First published in Great Britain in 1984 by
Darton, Longman and Todd Ltd
89 Lillie Road, London SW6 1UD

ISBN 0 232 51619 7

British Library Cataloguing in Publication Data

Pannenberg, Wolfhart
    Christian spirituality and sacramental community.
    1. Spirituality
    I. Title
    248.4   BV4501.2

ISBN–0–232–51619–7

Book design by Alice Derr

Printed in Great Britain by Anchor Brendon Ltd
Tiptree, Essex.

Contents

Preface

THE FIRST THREE chapters of this book contain the Taylor Lectures delivered at Yale Divinity School in 1977 under the title "Theological Issues in Christian Spirituality." Their printed form presents the original text, with only one paragraph added in the third chapter. The first two chapters deal with Christian spirituality in the proper sense—Chapter I in the form of a critique of a dominating type of traditional Protestant piety; Chapter II with reference to a recently emerging new focus in Christian worship across traditional barriers between churches. Chapter III crosses the bridge from church to society in discussing a political piety that has recently gained momentum in many churches of the Christian *oikoumene* although its Christian authenticity seems somewhat questionable.

Chapter IV offers an appraisal of secular culture concerning its significance for religious awareness. Chapter V considers what presents itself as a Buddhist response to the experience of secularity and to the place of subjectivity in it and compares that response to a Christian understanding of the religious roots of human selfhood.

WOLFHART PANNENBERG

I
Protestant Piety
and Guilt Consciousness

ACADEMIC theology works often at a distance from the emotional life of Christian piety. This does not necessarily indicate an alienation of the intellectual from involvement in religious life, although such alienation may not be rare. The specifically academic aloofness of theology is due in the first place to the spirit of historical investigation and of philosophical reflection. Both are required of the theologian, who may become immersed in historical detail and in developing a systematically coherent terminology as if these were ends in themselves. The reputation of a theologian as a scholar is largely measured by these technical skills. But authentic theology has always been distinguished beyond that by its ability to speak to central motifs of the Christian faith. These are not simply matters of doctrine, such as the Trinity, the cross and resurrection of Jesus Christ, God's kingdom, and faith itself. Such doctrinal issues are indeed related to the dynamic life of Christian faith, but when treated in separation from their experiential roots they can represent little but the deadwood of an old tradition. On the other hand, exegetical and doctrinal theology can embody an emotional commitment exhibiting a recognizable brand of accepted Christian piety, though it is rarely discussed as such and may not strike a familiar chord with everyone. The emotional response can be enthusiastic where a familiar form of piety underlies even harsh criticism of traditional positions—a combination that explains much of the success of the Bultmann school some decades ago. Observers who do not share the particular underlying pietistic attitude, of course, may wonder about its seeming violence. In conservative or iconoclastic fashion, the emotionally committed theologian enacts the correlation of doctrine and piety. But the theologian rarely investigates that piety itself and is even less prepared to recognize that it represents but one type of Christian piety among others.

In the more important forms of Christian spirituality we encounter the substructures of theology. The changing focus of Christian piety reveals a great deal about the history of Christian doctrine. It explains, for example, how at one time the incarnation was central; at another, the sacrificial death of Christ; and at yet another, justification by faith. Longing for participation in the eternal and weariness with the finite nature of this life were epitomized in the incarnation. The more severe and angry God seemed, the more important the question became as to how his claims could be satisfied and his anger appeased. The suffering of personal guilt feelings, coupled with a search for relief from an oppressive ecclesiastical hierarchy, made forgiveness of sin through justification by faith once more a key notion. In each of these major historical types of Christian piety, a complete interpretation of the world—although variable at many points—was implied. These not only represent the subjective attitudes that traditional psychology of religion dealt with under the name of piety, they also represent social and historical phenomena comparable to what has been called the spirit of an age, though their duration does not always coincide with the course of a particular age. They involve, first, a specific focus on Christian doctrine; second, a particular concept of the world of personal and social experience; and third, a characteristic style of life or, perhaps, a plurality of life-styles related to the peculiar focus on Christian doctrine and to the respective conception of human life in the world. Thus, the type of Christian piety that was shaped by the craving for participation in the eternal could correspond to a life-style of sacramental devotion or of monastic meditation. The type of piety that may be regarded as most typical of medieval Christianity was characterized by a concern for all sorts of mediation and intercession with God on behalf of sinners. Veneration of the saints, worship of relics, pilgrimages, the mediating and propitiatory function of the priest in celebrating the Eucharist, the propitiatory function of prayer, all these were so many elements that served the dominating concern of this type of piety. These different phenomena do not constitute, therefore, independent types of piety, but rather serve as contributory elements. In the new monastic orders of the thirteenth century, on the other hand, a new type of piety seems actually to have emerged, a piety concerned for immediacy to God. This concern became most powerful in a number of developments of the fourteenth century, in later Franciscan theology, in mysticism, and in the new Augustinianism. I regard the Reformation as emerging from that broader spiritual spectrum of the late Middle Ages. The Reformation represents still another form of the concern for immediacy in relation to God, a concern that always had been critical, at least implicitly, of the ecclesiastical system of mediation. Nevertheless, the Reformation finally produced its own type of piety, given perhaps its most classical expression in Luther's treatises on the freedom of a Christian: immediacy to God on the basis of the forgiveness of sin, and devotion to others by way of one's particular calling. The spiritual presence of Christ himself in the individual accounts for the dynamic of this Protestant piety.

It is not my purpose here to provide an *al fresco* sketch of the history of Christian piety through modern Christian humanism to the present day. What I want to ask now is whether the emergence and decay of historic types of piety can be understood. This is an important question because it uncovers the intrinsic relation of piety to the realities of life and consequently the possibility of testing and criticizing types of piety. Our pursuit of an answer will also yield criteria for new and more appropriate forms of Christian spirituality. A particular type of piety involves not only a specific theological focus and corresponding life-styles but also a particular conception of the human world, the world of human experience. It is at this point that the question of adequacy can be raised concerning a given type of piety. This question will be directed in this chapter to a case of particular contemporary importance, the decay of the pietistic transformation of Protestant piety or, more precisely, the critical dissolution of guilt consciousness.

Guilt consciousness is not, as such, a type of Christian piety. It has been pervasive in human experience and became an important element of many religious traditions. It was prominent in Judaism and rose to particular importance in Christianity because the Christian message is so closely connected with forgiveness of sins and redemption from the power of sin by the death of Jesus Christ. Nevertheless, guilt consciousness has become more influential in some forms of Christianity than in others, and increasingly so in Western Christianity. The Augustinian dogma of original sin was a specific product of Christianity in the West, but the development of penitential institutions and especially of a penitential mentality there also brought guilt consciousness into the focus of medieval piety. This was not a self-evident development.

In early Christianity, sin and guilt had been considered to be forgiven once and for all by the sacrament of Baptism.

The early Christian consciousness was characterized by the joyous experience of freedom from sin and death by communion with Christ. Toward the close of the second century, when the question arose whether Christians who committed serious offenses had to be excluded from the community or whether they should be given a second chance, the institution of a "second" penitence was created, second after Baptism, which had been the first one. In the ancient church, however, this second penitence, performed in public under severe conditions, continued to be the exception. It was only in the Western medieval church that regular penitential confession became a normal element in Christian life, and an increasingly pervasive element in Western Christian piety. It is well known that this development was furthered in the northern part of Europe by Irish and British monks who had cultivated the habit of mutual confession in their monasteries and extended it to the peoples they converted. Christians discovered themselves as living again under the power of sin. Entering their cathedrals, they passed between the wise and the foolish virgins at the portal, and beneath the representation of the Last Judgment; inside they were often faced by Christ as the last Judge looking down upon them from the apse. The underlying awareness of separation from God explains the craving for mediation that characterized so much medieval piety and remained the spiritual attitude the Reformation was concerned with. Although for the Reformers the message of the gospel was *liberation* from sin, anxiety, and guilt consciousness, yet it was addressed to precisely that mentality. For reasons to be discussed later, the glorious freedom of the Christian in Protestant piety could not rid itself of guilt consciousness. On the contrary, Protestant pietism would focus increasingly on the awareness of sin and guilt as a condition for genuine faith. One could be certain of salvation precisely to the extent that one identi-

fied oneself as a sinner completely dependent on the grace
of God, like the tax collector of Luke 18.

That a violent reaction against this mentality emerged in
the context of Protestantism was no accident. In his *Genealogy of Morals* (1887), Friedrich Nietzsche offered a devastating critique of the cultivation of guilt consciousness in the
Christian religion. The formerly pious young Nietzsche
revolted against the moralism and self-hatred of the pietistic
mentality in which he had been brought up, and he opposed
to its lamentations about sin and guilt the postulate of a new
self-assertive innocence. He derived the concepts of guilt,
duty, and conscience, not from a noble sense of high
morality as moralism did, but from the dirty ground of
economic obligation. He diagnosed bad conscience as a
mental disease, a case of interiorized aggression.[1] Above
all, he identified the biblical God as a projection of bad
conscience and claimed that the emergence of the Christian
God produced the maximum guilt consciousness on earth.
The destruction of this Christian God by atheism would
produce, according to Nietzsche, the liberation of humanity
from guilt consciousness. "Atheism and a sort of second
innocence belong together."[2]

Nietzsche regarded the "ascetic ideal" of Christianity
and its intensification of guilt consciousness as the most
catastrophic events in the "health history" of the European
mind.[3] In his view, the masochistic intensification of guilt
consciousness destroyed mental health, a criticism brought
forward later in a strikingly similar form by Sigmund Freud.
Although more pessimistic about human nature than Nietzsche and emphatic on the necessity of suppressing aggression if any culture is to develop, Freud characterized bad
conscience as a form of self-aggression under the pressure
of a socially conditioned superego.[4] He considered religion
a mass neurosis arising from guilt consciousness. Nietzsche
had used the term "neurosis" himself, and he had been the

first to trace the origin of religion back to the fear of the ancestors and of their power, connected with an awareness of indebtedness to them.[5] These ideas remind modern readers strikingly of Freud's *Totem and Taboo*, published in 1913. Freud did not attack the Christian religion as violently as Nietzsche had done. Concerning religion in general, however, he held views similar to Nietzsche's, developed on the basis of his criticism of the penitential mentality in Christian piety. Since Freud regarded guilt consciousness basically as self-aggression, he warned against excessively severe demands of the cultural superego,[6] which would drive the individual into neurosis and deprive a person of his or her chance of strengthening ego-identity.

The combined impact of Nietzsche and Freud in eroding traditional moral standards is hard to overestimate. Moral standards no longer appear as absolute norms but as internalized claims of society on the individual. If individual identity is felt to be threatened, society will be blamed and the norms may eventually be changed. But deep as their impact on the general culture has been, the effect of Nietzsche's and Freud's criticism on the credibility of traditional Christian piety has been even more fatal. The penitential mentality was unmasked as a mental disease, a particularly subtle and pernicious form of masochistic self-aggression. To the present day this criticism has not been taken with sufficient seriousness in Christian thought and in the life of the Christian churches. It confronts Christian theology with the question of whether God is indeed opposed to human identity and freedom and whether by the Christian faith people are trapped in neurotic attitudes. The pietistic type of Protestantism that gave rise to this criticism remains unfortunately particularly vulnerable to it. Since pietism has become so pervasively influential in many forms of Protestantism, the result is an emotional crisis that affects large segments of Protestant Christianity. Roman Catholicism seems also affected, though to a lesser degree, because penitential piety did not enjoy the same crucial importance there as it did in Protestantism.

Why is the penitential piety of Protestant pietism so vulnerable to the criticisms of Nietzsche and Freud? Because pietism, especially in its late revivalist forms, made meditation on guilt and sinfulness the basic and permanent condition for communion with God. But if consciousness of guilt is equivalent to nonidentity, this type of piety traps the individual in alienation. There is no escape from such alienation because there is combined with it a fantastic conception of self-identity in the name of salvation. Such a self-conception is doomed to remain fantastic because the permanent self-consciousness of personal sinfulness does not allow the individual to establish a new identity.

This problem did not always stand out clearly in Protestant history, although it is rooted in the central doctrines of the Reformers. The emphasis of the Reformation lay, of course, not on guilt consciousness as such, but rather on the liberation of the individual Christian from the anxieties of sinfulness and from the incertitudes of endless mediations. This liberation was based on the divine promise granted in Christ, spelled out in the divinely inspired Scriptures. It was available because of the immediacy of the Christian to the divine promise in Christ. To receive that freedom in Christ nothing was required beyond the acceptance of his promise, which happens whenever someone trusts in the promise, i.e., it happens in the act of faith.

From the beginning, however, a problem lurked in the new Protestant doctrine of Christian freedom, especially in its Lutheran form: the problem of the actualism of justification of faith. In Luther's own doctrine, to be sure, justification by faith was based on a real—and in some sense "mystical"—participation of the believer in Christ *extra nos*, outside ourselves. Luther thought that this takes place by the very act of faith as trust, since in entrusting ourselves *entirely* to someone we literally "leave" ourselves to that person. Our future, our life, is in the other's hands and depends on the kind of person the other is. Hence we share by faith in Jesus' life, spirit, and righteousness. On this level there emerges a continuous new existence of the believer *extra nos in Christo*, although within oneself one continues to be a sinner, again and again in need of forgiveness. Such forgiveness takes place when God counts our unity with Christ in faith against our intrinsic sinfulness. In theological terminology this was called *imputation* of the justice of Christ or *forensic justification*, because it consisted of an act of divine *judgment*. But if forensic justification is separated from the basic intuition of "mystical" participation in Christ by faith, then a peculiar *actualism* (or *extrinsicism*) results: We must accept the promise of divine forgiveness again and again, because we slide back into sin again and again. The shift toward such actualism occurred as early as in Melanchthon, whose rational sobriety had little access to the more profound mystical roots of Luther's thought. It vitiated the function of baptism (as constituting a continuous new life in Christ), because in spite of baptism sinfulness remains and divine forgiveness is needed again and again. It becomes an open question, then, how continuity in the new existence in Christ can be achieved and how the members of the congregation in the church are different—as Christians—from other sinners. In Luther's theology, baptism constituted the new existence *outside ourselves in Christ*, and Christian penitence was a continuous reappropriation of that baptism. But the relation of forensic justification to the emphasis on baptism soon faded in Christian piety and liturgy. In later Lutheran liturgies there is less reference to baptism than there should be, especially in connection with the liturgical confession of sin. Continuous Christian identity became a problem. Early pietism solved it through the concept of a once-for-all conversion and regeneration. The identity of a new life in Christ occurred *within* the individual rather than *outside ourselves* by faith in Christ, as Luther had taught, and the pietistic notion of a datable, once-for-all conversion providing a new life in Christ was always in acute danger of giving rise to a new self-righteousness. Revivalist movements since the middle of the eighteenth century stressed against that the need for repeated conversion and forgiveness, but this inevitably resulted in the actualism of an ever-repeated cycle of sin and forgiveness. This came to dominate Lutheran piety and other Protestant traditions as well.

The potential danger of such an actualism was not fully apparent as long as the authority of the Scriptures embodying the divine promise stood unchallenged, guaranteeing the continuity of Christian existence through the divine promise preceding every act of the individual. But when in the face of rationalistic criticism the authority of the Scriptures lost its public persuasiveness and had to be declared a matter of faith and of Christian experience, a reversion in the structure of reasoning became inevitable. The experience of one's own sinfulness became the criterion for the truth of the gospel, according to the classical dictum of F. A. G. Tholuck (1799–1877): *The revelation that solves the personal conflict within the individual in the best way is (for that person) the true one*. It is understandable, then, why evangelization again and again begins with the exposure of human sinfulness.

Notwithstanding the modification of the genuine perspective of the Lutheran Reformation along the way to revivalist pietism, there is a line of continuity from the doctrines of the former to the subjectivistic position of the latter. The Reformation—especially in its central doctrine of justification by faith—developed from theological reflection on the sacramental institution of penance in the medieval church and on its problems. By replacing the absolution of the priest with the promise of God and of Christ himself, the Reformation overcame the need for mediation of medieval Christianity and achieved a new immediacy to God in Christ. At the same time—and by the same step—the meaning of penitence was extended far beyond that particular sacramental act so as to permeate every aspect of Christian existence. The penitential mentality became ubiquitous. This came to a characteristic expression in the overall conception of Lutheran theology in terms of the distinction between law and gospel.

This bipolar structure was discovered in the Scriptures, especially in Paul. But in Luther's perspective the two terms did not indicate—as in Paul's letters—two successive periods in the divine history of revelation, but rather two coordinate principles of the Christian life. The coordination of these two principles is fully understandable only from the point of view of the medieval sacrament of confession or penitence: the *law* corresponds to the divine commandments which the confessor calls to the attention of the penitent in order to stimulate the remembrance of particular sins. The *gospel* and its proclamation corresponds to the words of absolution. If one considers how many Protestant sermons have been structured more or less by application of the same coordinate principles of law and gospel, it becomes evident how pervasive the influence of penitential piety has been in Protestant tradition. Pietism simply carried on at this point. It had only to exploit further the psychological sequence leading from contrite recognition of human misery to eager acceptance of the divine promise liberating one from that misery: a road prepared in advance by Melanchthon.

Although in this penitential piety concern with human sinfulness served as the starting point on the side of experience, it did not originally intensify self-aggression or deprive the individual of human identity. On the contrary, the dynamic of this conception was to convey a new and solid identity to the individual, in Christian liberty, independent of all human authority. The Reformation achieved this under conditions of the medieval penitential attitude and as a transformation of that attitude, thus exemplifying how a type of piety implies an interpretation of the world of human experience, a historical system of life. As long as the medieval penitential attitude could be taken for granted, the liberating effect of the Protestant conception of Christian freedom through justification by faith continued to work. Nevertheless, consciousness of personal sinfulness not only provided the historical opportunity for a new formulation of Christian freedom but was also its systematic presupposition. A problem, therefore, was bound to arise when this presupposition lost its self-evident status because of changes in anthropology that would make divine law seem less threatening and more benevolent. Under these changing conditions perpetuating the law-and-gospel scheme of Protestant piety meant preserving the presupposed penitential mentality through that scheme itself. The preaching of the law had first to *produce* a guilt consciousness that otherwise would not arise. And then, in a historical world of a more optimistic anthropology, the consciousness of sin had also to be *re*produced continuously by the threatening power of the divine law, although it was no longer self-evident that the divine will was indeed so threatening.

This growing split between *piety* and what could be taken for granted as human *reality* characterizes the march of pietism into neurosis. Inevitably the message of Christian freedom was obscured by the increasing strain of reforging the consciousness of sin by violent blows with the hammer of divine law. The increasing labor of thus securing the guilt consciousness needed for proclaiming the gospel of gratuitous forgiveness produced a specifically Protestant form of self-righteousness. The good Protestant knows that the only chance for righteousness is to put oneself in the place of the sinner, of the tax collector, rather than that of the Pharisee. The consciousness of sin must be kept at a boil. It usually goes unnoticed that these very efforts put the good Protestant in the place of the Pharisee. Protestant self-righteousness does not necessarily require good works; the ultimately crucial point is to manage one's emotional household. The dogs of self-aggression, of course, that must be used to this end may easily get out of hand. In any event, the glorious freedom once connected with justification by faith has withdrawn to a great distance, except where the modern Protestant succeeds in restricting guilt consciousness to Sundays for the sake of strengthened self-assurance of being like the repentant tax collector. Only its perverse use renders it bearable. Protestant theologians and churchmen alike have asked themselves repeatedly in recent decades why justification by faith has almost become a dead issue. One answer is that under an altered anthropology and ethical consciousness the Lutheran scheme of law and gospel developed an alienating thrust. One has to call it counterproductive, if its achievements are measured by the standard of the Reformers' idea of Christian freedom. This does not mean that the call to conversion, the call to return to God, is meaningless in the present world. On the contrary, there have been few periods in Western history when the call for a return to God was more timely and more urgent. But the return to God in our age is not in the first place a matter of individual morality. Before it is that, it is a matter of caring for God, a matter of concern for the transcendent in the understanding of the realities of life, not only for oneself as an individual but also in society. As long as the idea of God has little to do with the way we think about our everyday activities, about the responsibilities and recreations implicit in the institutional texture of our society, moral conversion remains an unnatural imposition on our lives, relevant mainly to our emotional economy and that often in a neurotic way. If the point in conversion is to be wholly and perfectly with God, then most of us must begin differently, i.e., by reforming our thought in order to overcome the secularist emancipation of everyday life from God. And we must keep in mind that such conversion cannot be achieved by the isolated individual but involves a transformation of society. There may occur individual situations where even today conversion demands first of all a change in the moral strategy of life, but such cases are exceptions rather than the typical form of conversion required by our age. Normally, it is not just the moral strategy but the whole outlook of life that must change. And this can be achieved only by recasting our interpretation of the world and of our place in it in terms of the sovereignty of God and of his kingdom.

Most unpromising for the prospect of a lively Christian spirituality is the habit of preaching moral conversion from the pulpit. This is rooted in the penitential mentality of the Protestant tradition and is continually reaffirmed by the tenacious survival of the law-and-gospel scheme in Protestant homiletics. Such a mentality in the preacher serves merely to pin down baptized Christians to a contrite consideration of their sinfulness. It is as if they were sitting not within the church but without. It achieves little more than to support a vicious circle of indeterminate guilt consciousness and a self-righteous faith in justification. That is the direct effect of confronting a congregation with moral demands in vague generalities that cannot readily be applied to individual life situations. General consideration of ethical norms belongs to discussion of cultural foundations, which, however, cannot be simply moral, but finally must be religious. Moral generalities, because they are so sweeping, can produce only resignation, which through identification with the publican feeds an equally empty belief in justification. Another side to this deterioration of justifying faith into empty ritual is that preaching moral conversion contributes to the continuous ruin of the credibility of Christian language. Next Sunday, after all, the same sermon will be heard again, since the preacher obviously does not feel that this Sunday the word of God effectively achieved conversion in the community. But, of course, the congregation also knows that this is just the style of preaching. No one anticipates any significant change.

As the need for genuine conversion is not denied by this criticism of guilt consciousness in Christian piety, neither is the doctrine of human sinfulness called into question thereby. Christian theology need not diagnose bad conscience as mental disease, particularly as self-aggression, but the challenge of psychological description cannot be evaded either. We must never forget that baptized Christians are, in principle, liberated from the power of sin, although they do continue to be tempted by the egocentricity that Paul called "flesh." There are relapses into sin, and consequently, there is individual guilt. These need to be addressed, not in vague generalities but in specifics inappropriate for mention in the public sermon. Cases, however, of corporate failure of the Christian congregation in the context of its society should be dealt with in the sermon, though not on a primarily moralistic basis. These require descriptive clarification of the place of the Christian community within its social world. This descriptive approach also applies to the question of sin in general as an aspect of anthropology. As long as sin is basically understood as failure to comply with divine commandments, even if that failure is traced back to unbelief as its root, the theological doctrine of sin confirms the psychological diagnosis of the consciousness of sin as a result of self-aggression. This suspicion can be overcome only if the concept of sin can be related to a more fundamen-

tal nonidentity in the human situation, one that is not a
consequence of moral norms but prior to all moral reflection. There is, indeed, in the structure of human behavior a
tension between egocentricity and self-transcendence, a
tension that disrupts the human identity of the individual.
Identity is not something primordially given, but a goal to be
obtained only by overcoming nonidentity. And if human
identity is bound up with the religious question, then there
may be good reason to call that nonidentity which is
indigenous to the human condition "sin." Such a descriptive theory of human sinfulness cannot be said to provide a
paradigm for self-aggression, because it begins with a description of the human condition rather than with moral
norms. It is this human condition which must be overcome
in order to achieve genuine self-identity. Thus we can
indeed respond to psychological criticism of Christian piety,
but not on the basis of the law-and-gospel scheme of
traditional pentitentialism. As long as that scheme continues
in effect, the chances for theology and piety to survive the
assaults of psychological criticism are bleak, and it is safe to
predict that cases of neurotic piety will reappear for some
time to come.

As the concept of law does not promote the awareness of
personal sinfulness presupposed by the traditional penitential piety, so the penitential scheme of law and gospel is also
an inappropriate instrument for motivating conversion to
the Christian faith. Even if individuals become aware that
they lack genuine human identity, they will not necessarily
feel themselves driven to the gospel, since there are many
other options that promise to fulfill the search for meaning,
even other religious options. Without resorting to a strategy
of inflaming neurotic processes like the terrors of conscience, there is no longer any easy way leading from the
law to the gospel. Rather, the illuminative power of the
Christian tradition, in comparison with other approaches to

the quest for human meaning must be diligently investigated. This means that the traditional penitential pietism, its
lasting influence in Protestant theology and spirituality
notwithstanding, is unfit as a truly contemporary form of
Christian piety that could claim to embody the spirit of
liberation that has motivated and accompanied the gospel
proclamation throughout history.

Such a negative judgment, finally, does not mean we must
reject the Protestant doctrine of justification by faith. In late
medieval penitential piety this doctrine effectively expressed Christian freedom from the power of sin and death,
as well as from all human authority, through acceptance of
the divine promise. We must realize, however, that this
concept of Christian freedom was couched in the language
of penitential piety and therefore remained bound by its
limitations. This is indicated especially by the actualism of
the Reformers' conception of justifying faith, particularly
when it was no longer embedded in Luther's vision of real,
"mystical" participation in Jesus Christ as its basis. Trust in
the promised righteousness outside ourselves in Christ
(*extra nos in Christo*) presupposes sinfulness as the intrinsic
condition of the believer.[7] In the perspective of a purely
forensic conception of justification, therefore, believers
must turn again and again beyond themselves in their
concern for their salvation, and thus continue to relate to
themselves as sinners. Because of the split between the
extrinsic and the intrinsic aspects of the self, Protestant
believers could not arrive at a unified self-concept that
would allow for a continuous life history based on transformation by Christ, beginning with baptism. Instead of continuity, Protestant believers were forced time after time to
turn away from their corrupt and sinful nature to that
justification to be obtained from the promise of Christ alone.
This, again, gave rise to peculiarly Protestant forms of self-
righteousness and hypocrisy, as it did to pietistic subjectiv-

ism when the presupposition of justifying faith in the contrite experience of one's personal sinfulness had to be secured by recourse to the divine law. The consequence of this development is that the fundamental idea of the Reformation, the freedom of the believer through participation in Christ, can be rescued only by separating it from penitential piety. Otherwise the believer could not avoid that self-aggression which prevents the formation of a genuine self-identity. If there is to be a new manifestation of the spirit of liberation and the joy of being redeemed from an inauthentic life (things whose absence Nietzsche so sarcastically noted in Christian attitudes), a break with the traditional penitential mentality is as inevitable as a quest for new forms of Christian piety and life. A personal view of how this might take shape will be presented in the next chapter.

II
Eucharistic Piety—
A New Experience
of Christian Community

CRITICISM is easier than reconstruction. What new manifestation should we expect of the spiritual freedom of the Christian, if it is to be delivered from bondage to penitential piety? People are prone to look for something new, and all too often the new lacks the profound, substantial meaning enshrined in traditional forms. What is most significantly new, therefore, sometimes occurs as a new look at something one has known long since. The rediscovery of the Eucharist may prove to be the most important event in Christian spirituality of our time, of more revolutionary importance than even the liturgical renewal may realize.

New types of piety cannot be created at will, and certainly not by theoretical design. But there may be long-standing alternatives available for a dominant type of piety as well as seminal developments that could provide fertile grounds for the emergence of a new type. The adequacy of these can be checked for their relevance to the needs of a particular age. This may be done appropriately by contrasting their potential with the strength and the shortcomings of the options already available.

The strength of penitential pietism consisted in its support of those who felt themselves planted in the unshakable ground of the divine promise in Jesus Christ. But the price of this strength was self-aggression, and in time this price has increasingly come to seem excessive. Another limitation has been its virtual individualism. At first glance, this may seem unfair to say, since pietism has been a major incentive for creating new religious associations, always providing a strong impulse to form small groups of the truly faithful, as well as a powerful motivation for missionary work and evangelization. Nevertheless, pietistic and revivalist spirituality has been concerned primarily with individual salvation. The fact that there was also a strong concern for others—that is, for *their* individual salvation—does not disprove but confirms this. The other person was seen as another individual, wrestling similarly with the question of his or her eternal salvation. Associations of like-minded individuals sprang up, with even an ecumenical enthusiasm, especially in the early phases of the pietistic movement, because of the widespread aversion to theological theory and confessional controversy. But an authentic conception of the Christian church was hard to develop on this basis, a conception of the church as one, holy, apostolic, and catholic body, for the body of Christ is more than an association of independent individuals.

It could be shown that Christian humanism, the other main type of modern Protestant piety, suffers from the same problem. Although Christian humanists are concerned that their Christian views of human destiny and dignity be publicly acceptable, they are often content to invoke this subjective attachment to the Christian tradition to authenticate the Christian character of their views. Characteristically, Christian humanism has been far less productive in generating religious communities and churches than the pietistic and revivalist movement has been. If the Christian humanist belongs to a church, it is often an ambiguous relationship, because the spiritual life is concerned to be basically a matter of private discretion.

The convergence of the two attitudes in individualism is revealing. It may appear today as a weakness, a limitation they have in common, but it has been at the same time the mark of their modernity. Both occupied precisely the one place modern society had left to religion, that of private belief and private commitment. This corresponds to the modern contention that the institutions of public life are independent of religious beliefs. Agreement with this prejudice exhibits both an element of strength and of weakness in those two typical forms of modern piety: The element of strength derives from compliance with the modern conception of religion and society, the element of weakness is in Christian acceptance of the limitations of purely subjective truth, corresponding to the inability of modern Christianity to understand and expose the inevitably delusive character of a separation between religion and politics. Modern Christianity, therefore, has been characterized by an ability to transform modern society in such a way as to produce a new theonomous culture. That the two most influential forms of modern Protestant spirituality have been unable to create such a theonomous culture is due as much to unfavourable external conditions as to intrinsic limitations.

On the contemporary scene, there is a worldwide trend toward a redefinition of the interrelation of individual and society. It is plainly evident in the rise of socialism, Marxist or otherwise. But it comes also to the fore in Western youth movements and the counterculture, as well as in theoretical descriptions of the constitutive importance of the social setting for individual identity. At the same time traditional social structures like the family on the one hand and the established forms of political organization on the other are losing ground, their influence on the formation of individual identity eroding. Thus, there is a vague but profound yearning for more authentically human forms of community and social life. This emotional desire induces many people to commit themselves to socialist ideas, programs, and organizations in spite of the disappointing and sometimes disastrous results this century has experienced from socialist experiments. The experience of two generations teaches that socialism in its various forms tends to maximize bureaucratic structure and often favors oppressive forms of government. But many people are not ready to learn this lesson because of the emotional and basically religious urge to believe in the possibility of an unalienated human society that would allow the individual to participate in a renewed communal life.

Others prefer the warmer climate of small groups where life and resources are really shared. Still others seek relief from individual isolation in sexual communion. If it is the profound desire for community that people attempt to satisfy in all these ways, they will often be disappointed, because they ask too much of a group experience or of interpersonal communion, more than it can possibly give. The reason for this, presumably, is that the need people attempt to satisfy by seeking the experience of human community is basically a religious one.

It may not be too hard, then, to imagine a type of piety that might meet the religious needs of our time. A number of experiments in creating new communal forms of religious life have been, indeed, remarkably successful. Most of the Protestant examples, however, remain indebted to the old penitential pietism, their appeal being thus limited to those who are still approachable through it. Further, small religious groups suffer from some of the same limitations as other groups do concerning the experience of a community that would constitute the identity of the individual. Lest the spirit of the group be suffocated by individual inadequacies and rivalries, it needs a more universal concern, and the most universal form of it relates to the community of all human beings, to what has been called the global village.

This concern is articulated sometimes by appealing to a sense of direct personal responsibility for people in other continents, thus generating some admirable activities indeed. But such appeal can also result in moralistic self-delusion. In any event, the global village that would unite all human beings is a powerful symbol, and we should appreciate its spiritual power more than we usually do. It is only by symbols and symbolic language that the larger community to which we belong is present in our experiences and activities. The flag, the national anthem, and the ceremonies of a national holiday let the unity of a nation become visibly present on particular occasions. In another way the public offices in a society possess a symbolic meaning that is indispensable for their authority, because only insofar as an officeholder represents the unity of the people will the authority of that person be obeyed. Throughout history, such symbolism conveyed to individuals a sense of serving a comprehensive community, stimulating people to stronger devotion than the attachment to a closer but more limited group usually produces.

The Christian church is a symbolic community. It is not only that the church uses symbols that unite all Christians, like the cross, or that the ministries of the church are symbolic in representing the people as political offices do. In the case of the church the community itself is symbolic. The Christian community symbolizes another community, the community of all human beings in a society of perfect justice and peace, the global village, the kingdom of God. The Christian knows that the global village is not a reality that could be already at hand, nor is it possible to establish it either by human government or by political revolution that inevitably produces another form of human government, in which some will be again in charge to administer the order of society over the rest of its members. Human government always reserves political power or at least its legitimate use to a small number of individuals, and is therefore always stained by some element of injustice. The hope for a society of perfect justice and peace has therefore been expressed, in the biblical tradition, as the hope that the kingdom of God will replace every form of human governance. Because this global village is not yet at hand as a political reality, it can be present only in a symbolic way, and it is present in the symbolic community of the Christian church. It is also present in the chosen people of Israel, who were chosen to the blessing of all humanity and, of course, in whom the Christian church has its roots. But while the Jewish people are a particular people who acquired a symbolic function in human history, the Christian church was constituted from the outset as a symbolic entity. There is no reason for the existence of the church except to symbolize the future of the divine kingdom that Jesus came to proclaim. This explains in what specific sense worship is in the center of life of the church: The worship of the Christian community anticipates and symbolically celebrates the praise of God's glory that will be consummated in the eschatological renewal of all creation in the new Jerusalem.

As a symbolic community the church is distinct from the political organization of the state. This distinction does not mean that the church cares for the religious needs of individual persons, while the state administers the public weal. It is not a distinction of different fields or of different fundamental concerns. Rather, the existence of the Christian church is related to the social and political destiny of human life as much as the state is, but in a different way, through symbolic representation. The very existence of the church entails, therefore, the contention that the state does not exhaust or even ultimately accomplish the political destiny of human life. The mere existence of the church delimits the claims of any present political organization on the life of its members. This explains why tensions have constantly developed between churches and governments where the authorities were not willing to accept the limitation on their claims implied by the very existence of the Christian church. The church differs from the state in that the political destiny of humanity is represented by the church in its ultimacy, though in symbolic form, while the state directly embodies the political organization of society and therefore remains provisional. The church is also provisional, but in another way. In the new Jerusalem, there will be no temple any longer, no church. The provisional status of the church is entailed in its symbolic character, notwithstanding the ultimacy of the subject matter that is symbolized in its existence. This symbolic character penetrates every institution in and activity of the church, and if it fails in that symbolism which is its very essence, the church degenerates into an authoritarian, even tyrannical agency. The dogma of the church is symbolic, and when its symbolic nature is forgotten, then the dogma is perverted into coercive uniformity. The episcopal ministry of the church symbolizes and thereby represents its universal unity in the life of a local congregation. If the basically symbolic nature of the ministry happens to be forgotten, then the ministry is likely to arrogate to itself tyrannical powers, if only in the form of bureaucratic competence. The thoroughly symbolic nature of the liturgy is more obvious, although it is rarely expounded consistently and in every detail. If the symbolic nature of the liturgy is forgotten, however, it becomes a dead ritual, performed as a cheerless duty. But even the social and charitable activities of the church or churches are basically symbolic, as Jesus' own activities of healing the sick and feeding the poor were. If the symbolic character of the charitable activities of the church is not observed, the church may still not assume the role of economic preceptor of the world. Fortunately, this remains a remote possibility. Nevertheless, if there is no awareness of the symbolic character of charitable activities, the church is likely to overlook the fact that human beings do not live on bread alone. The church may feel obliged, then, to promote an empty moralism that overstresses the possibilities of the church and of its members and hence primarily serves to nourish the guilt consciousness of the individual Christian.

The nature of the church, then, is thoroughly symbolic, and not only its perversions but also its lack of illuminative and inspirational power are largely due to poor apprehension of that symbolism. To restore the feeling for the thoroughly symbolic nature of the church means to recover its spiritual reality. Instead of using the term "symbolic," I could speak of the sacramental nature of the church, since the term "sacrament" has been defined as efficacious sign or symbol, *signum efficax*.[8] The church's institutions and activities exercise their specific effectiveness by way of their symbolic power. To call something "symbolic" does not deem it ineffective, although this is how a tenacious prejudice would see it. Symbols can be more effective than rocks or bullets. Since an effective symbol has been called a sacrament, I could speak of a sacramental as well as of a symbolic nature of the church. Since in some Protestant ears the term "sacramental" bears a number of negative connotations—originating partly in earlier periods of the history of theology, partly in psychological prejudice—I would rather avoid it. There is no difference in meaning here, however.

This long discussion of the church as a symbolic community has been necessary to set the stage for evaluating the Eucharist and its place in the life of the church and of the churches. The central significance of the Eucharist in that life can only be questioned if the symbolic nature of the church as a whole is insufficiently considered. That, of course, indicates a serious deformation in the theological conception of the church, a charge against which the ecclesiologies of the Reformers cannot be entirely defended. The Reformers placed the proclamation of the gospel in the center of the church's life in a fashion closely connected with the dominant influence of penitential piety, thus according a dangerously authoritarian character to the function of the preacher. The Reformers may be excused in this, however, in that the doctrine of the church was generally not far developed in their time. Further, in Luther's early writings there was a brief moment when the central importance of the Eucharist was recognized, though later it came to be subordinated to the sermon as structured on the lines of penitential piety according to the scheme of law and gospel.

That brief moment occurred in 1519 when Luther published his "Sermon on the Sacrament of the Holy and True Body of Christ"—which was rather a treatise. Here Luther pointed out that the meaning of this sacrament is a twofold communion: first the communion of the believer with Christ, and secondly the communion among all those who enjoy such unity with Christ and thus form the one body of Christ.[9] His argument clearly recognized the ecclesial character of the Eucharist. Luther even reapplied a powerful image from the Didache (9, 4), saying that as many grains of wheat came together to form the single loaf of bread that is being broken and distributed in the sacrament, so the faithful are joined together in the sacrament to form one bread, one cup, one body in communion with Christ.[10] This passage indicates a profound understanding of the ecclesial symbolism of the Eucharist. But only one year later, in the "Sermon on the New Testament or on Holy Mass," 1520, the direction of the argument had changed. A consideration that had already been present in 1519, but in a more subordinate way, became dominant now: the interpretation of the words of institution as divine promise given in order to assure the individual of the forgiveness of his or her

sins.[11] Thus the Eucharist was made subservient to penitential piety. The broader spectrum of its meaning was no
longer present.

The unique significance of the Eucharist in the life of the
church is indeed intimately connected with its ecclesial
symbolism. There is no other place or event in the worship
of the church where the very foundation of its life can be
comparably commemorated and symbolized, as well as
reenacted, than in the event of celebration and communion.
As Luther recognized, the essence of the church is communion of the faithful on the basis of the communion with Jesus
Christ that each individual member shares. Every celebration of the Eucharist reenacts the reality that constitutes the
foundation of the church, and that happens not only in the
sense of memorial but also in the symbolic power of the
Eucharist, where the essence of the church itself is alive,
present, and effective. Lest I be unclear on this point, let me
put it more bluntly: *The Eucharist, not the sermon, is in the
center of the church's life.* The religious individuality that
produces itself in the pulpit, while telling us that it is really
the word of God that we hear, should not be the center of
worship. The sermon should serve, not dominate, in the
church. It should serve the presence of Christ which we
celebrate in the Eucharist.

The centrality of the Eucharist in the life of the church
and in our worship has been obscured and weakened by our
failure appropriately to understand and appreciate eucharistic symbolism. This insensibility, however, seems due largely to the predominance of penitential piety even in attitudes
to and interpretations of the Eucharist. There has been a
Roman Catholic distortion of the meaning of the Eucharist
in shaping the eucharistic liturgy into a propitiatory sacrifice
offered for our sins. There has been also a Calvinistic
distortion, wherein the Eucharist was celebrated as a presentation of the holy congregation, sinners not admitted.

But there has been also a Lutheran distortion of the meaning of the Eucharist, in celebrating it primarily as a visible and touchable assurance to the individual of the forgiveness of sins. All these different distortions of the symbolic structure of the eucharistic liturgy are related in different ways to the impact of penitential piety.

This comes especially to the fore in the traditional notion of unworthy communion. When Paul warned against unworthy communion (I Cor. 11:27ff.) he was not concerned with the intrinsic moral condition of the individuals and with a corresponding need for confession and absolution prior to Holy Communion, but rather with a lack of appreciation for the communal implications in the celebration of the Eucharist. Forgiveness of sins is exhibited in the Eucharist itself. Therefore it obscures the meaning of the Eucharist to make absolution a prior condition for participation. One should rather be concerned with the social obligations following from that participation.

Typical forms of eucharistic doctrine in the churches did not always sufficiently appreciate the central importance of the communal symbolism of the Eucharist in expressing a twofold community, first of the individual participants themselves. This communal element is the most important dimension of eucharistic symbolism. A second dimension may be called the *sacrificial* one, and it closely corresponds to the first. The devotion of Jesus Christ in giving himself to the world constitutes the community with him which the believer receives, and that devotion to Jesus Christ also constitutes community among the faithful, because Jesus was sent not only for the private benefit of this or that individual but to save the world. Here the sacrificial element in the Eucharist already points to a third dimension of eucharistic symbolism, the eschatological one. Jesus' mission to the world at large points to an ultimate completion that has not yet been achieved. But before we investigate the full dynamic of the eucharistic symbolism, a few closer considerations in relation to the use of the word "sacrificial" are appropriate. If this means Jesus' devotion to his mission and to the people he had been sent to save, then the traditional image of Jesus' offering himself as a sacrifice to the Father in order to appease his wrath against his sinful creatures, is misleading. It is not merely wrong, since in his devotion to the people he was commissioned to save Jesus indeed devoted his life to the Father and offered his life to the Father, who had commissioned him with that mission to the benefit of sinful humanity. In an intellectual situation saturated with the sacrificial imagery of the Jewish tradition, as seems to have been the case in Hellenistic Judaism, it is understandable that Jesus' death was interpreted in that language. It proved misleading, however, in that this imagery obscured the fact that in the New Testament it was not so much God who had to be reconciled, but the world. And this reconciliation, not of an angry God, but of the world, was the direction of Jesus' devotion to a divine mission that ipso facto was his devotion to the people he had been sent to save. The sacrificial devotion of Jesus in facing his death, therefore, was at the root of the eucharistic communion which he created in celebrating the meal.

In the present period of Christian history, a new sensitivity for the communal meaning of the Eucharist is developing. If this were not the case, one could not understand the increasing participation in eucharistic communion, a tendency that has been observed not only in Catholic churches but also among Protestants, even in Germany. I say "even" in Germany, because it is somewhat behind the development of world Protestantism toward reappropriating the eucharistic liturgy to the regular Protestant service. There is a development to this effect, however, in many Protestant churches, although it is by no means universal and complete. The psychological barriers of a narrow and defensive mentality that regards a eucharistic service as a Roman or Greek Catholic peculiarity, are still strong in the Protestant world. It will take some time and a great deal of commitment for that mentality to vanish. On the other hand, there is a new eucharistic sensibility spreading throughout the Protestant world, closely related to the sense of Christian community. Hence, it is not by accident that some of the more visible expressions of this new sensibility have come from the World Council of Churches in a series of documents increasingly emphasizing the central importance of the celebration of the Eucharist for the process of Christian reunification. Further, with remarkable determination the Second Vatican Council in its Constitution on the Sacred Liturgy emphasized the communal character of eucharistic worship. Here the Roman Catholic Church met a classical demand of the Reformation, and it should sadden a Protestant theologian to think that the Reformation, while in accordance with its biblical orientation emphasizing the right principle, i.e., the communal or congregational character of the Eucharist, nevertheless failed to develop a new and powerful eucharistic piety. This has been left to our own time.

One of the most promising manifestations of such a new eucharistic spirituality has been the tendency toward intercommunion which we have seen since the Second Vatican Council. Unfortunately, the spiritual significance of this movement has been little understood by many church leaders. Some of their objections were not without good reasons, to be sure. Even if eucharistic communion does not only express a prior unity in faith and order, it must entail church unity, and if there are serious reasons which prevent that unity, the joint celebration of the Eucharist seems premature. On the other hand, the experiences of eucharistic communion across the barriers that still divide the churches has created in many cases a new sense of Christian unity that in the final result may well contribute to the reunification of the churches. Moreover, the dynamic character of such experiences disclosed to many Christians for the first time the spiritual power of sacramental performance and participation. Catholic bishops, who often reacted defensively to the spread of irregular eucharistic celebration and communion, did not always appreciate the spiritual significance of these experiences, particularly where among Protestant participants these had bearing on a new sacramental spirituality.

For centuries there was little if any eucharistic piety in most Protestant churches. The penitential mentality and conception of worship, particularly of the sermon as viewed by that penitential mentality, overlaid it psychologically and pushed it aside in the liturgical life of the churches. Eucharistic piety came to be regarded by many Protestants as a distinguishing mark of Catholic Christianity. The understanding of eucharistic worship in the Roman Catholic Church did indeed emphasize elements that the Reformation rejected, especially the interpretation of the Eucharist as a sacrificial offering presented to God by the priest, if only in sacramental form. In this respect, the emerging eucharistic spirituality of our own time differs profoundly from the eucharistic piety of former periods, not only in the Protestant churches but also in the Roman Catholic Church. The difference is that the spirit of the new eucharistic piety is thoroughly communal. In the postmedieval form of Roman Catholic eucharistic piety the communion of the congregation could be separated from the celebration of the Eucharist, since the liturgical action centered altogether in the sacrificial offering and in the worship of the presence of Christ in the elements. This traditional kind of eucharistic piety, therefore, represented one form among others of the concern for mediation rather than an independent type of piety. In the contemporary scene, however, there is a chance that the eucharistic piety conceived on the basis of the communal symbolism of the Eucharist may become the organizing center of a new ecclesial spirituality that liberates the Christian from individualism on the one hand and from an overemphasis on the legal authority of ecclesiastical institutions on the other. The sacrificial dimension may be integrated into such a conception of eucharistic symbolism along the lines indicated earlier. The same applies to the eschatological dimension of eucharistic symbolism. It is only this eschatological dimension that provides the universal outlook that is inherent in eucharistic experience and that embraces society at large and all humankind. Hitherto the new eucharistic spirituality remained ecclesiocentric, despite the fact that the eschatological dimension has been emphasized by New Testament exegesis as well as by theology. We can expect that the eschatological perspective will eventually overcome a narrowly ecclesiocentric attitude. Only under such conditions can an emerging eucharistic spirituality display the spiritual power to constitute a new historical type of Christian piety. Only a broad conception of eucharistic symbolism as relating to the destiny of all humanity can achieve this, because nothing that is not relevant to all humanity can constitute the human identity of the individual.

The eschatological dimension of eucharistic symbolism first appeared in connection with sacrificial devotion as a constitutive principle of the twofold eucharistic communion. The divine commission to which Jesus devoted his life was not related to a secluded religious community, but to the world, i.e., to every single human being, and it related to the world in order to proclaim the advent of the kingdom of God as the ultimate future of all humanity. When Jesus insisted that in his proclamation and in the reaction of his followers the kingdom of God becomes a reality already present, he made clear that he was not talking about some distant future, but that the reality he talked about came to power in the event of his proclamation. Correspondingly, Jesus celebrated the presence of the eschatological kingdom in the simple form of the meals he took together with his disciples, but also with Pharisees, with "tax collectors and sinners" who by the intrinsic symbolism of the joint meal were accepted by Jesus as candidates and citizens of the future kingdom of God. As in the Jewish prophetic tradition the ultimate hope for a human community of perfect peace and justice in the divine kingdom to come had been expressed in the image of a meal, so Jesus anticipated that eschatological glory in celebrating the meal with the disciples and those who became his disciples on the occasion of their participation. The Christian Eucharist is the continuation of this symbolic action of Jesus himself, enriched by the sacrificial symbolism that was connected with the tradition of the last occasion when Jesus "in the night in which he was betrayed" celebrated the meal with his disciples. Even within this specific tradition an explicit reference to the eschatological dimension is present in Jesus' words that from this time on he will "not drink again of the fruit of the vine" (Mark 14:25) before the kingdom will be fully present.

For the eschatological perspective of eucharistic symbolism the symbolic performance of the eucharistic liturgy and communion anticipates the ultimate completion of the social destiny of all human life. This serves as a testimony to the fact that the present structures of social and political life do not adequately realize the common destiny of the human race, which will be fully achieved only when God's rule replaces all human rule. Thus, in eucharistic liturgy and communion the freedom of Christians from the claims of society comes to expression together with their communion with and allegiance to the Messiah, the King of the eschatological future. Freedom from the claims of society does not mean, however, that the Christian will emigrate spiritually

from the social world. Rather, that awareness of freedom is
conveyed by participation in the symbolic presence of the
ultimate attainment of human community, which in our
political and social reality remains a mere promise the
fulfillment of which can be claimed only by deluding the
people. Because eucharistic symbolism confirms the social
destiny of humankind, it also encourages and inspires
political commitment for the sake of peace and justice. In
connection with such commitment, as it continues the
sacrificial devotion of Jesus Christ, the symbolism of the
Eucharist is experienced more intensively than otherwise.
But in the framework of eucharistic piety, such social and
political commitment can never be what the Eucharist
symbolizes. On the contrary, the symbolism by far exceeds
whatever social activities it may inspire. Making it subservient to the actualities of political programs perverts it. The
human predicament of social life is not ultimately realized in
the present political order of society, but is celebrated in the
worship of the church, if only in the form of the symbolic
presence of the kingdom to come. The awareness that in the
liturgy of the church there is symbolically present what all
social and political struggle is about without its definite
achievement, is absolutely crucial to the significance of the
eucharistic liturgy. Without this dimension, the eucharistic
liturgy degenerates into a self-contained, ecclesiocentric
ritual, if not into a self-delusive reassurance of private
participation in the salvation acquired by Jesus Christ.

The Eucharist manifests the mystery of the church, the
communion of believers united by the communion of each
with Christ, and symbolizes the eschatological unity of all
humanity. The power of this symbolism, however, is seriously impaired today by the dividedness of Christianity.
How is the world to believe that the power of Christ's
presence in the unity of his disciples symbolizes the future
of a united humanity, as long as Christians continue to be

divided into different churches, each of which claims exclusively to represent "the" church? Presently many Christians think the mutual exclusivity and intolerance of the churches has been sufficiently overcome so that further steps toward organic unity of the churches no longer seem urgent. Such self-deceptive complacency underestimates the continuous impact of mutual exclusivity. If it were no longer operative, the churches would admit each other's members to communion, but the continuing separation of the churches is nowhere more obvious and unbearable than in their mutual exclusion from the Eucharist instituted by Christ as a celebration of the unity of his disciples in their communion with himself. The body of Christ has been divided and dismembered. The scandal is not that there continue to be organizational differences or a plurality of organized churches. The scandal is that the churches to this day do not accept each other in the community of love that they celebrate in their Eucharist. The eucharistic presence of the Lord ought not to be made a means of self-authentication for each separate church. Each time the Eucharist is celebrated in one of our churches the Lord is present in judgment on his divisive and unfaithful followers.

But even this dark side of the eucharistic experience testifies to its liberating power. It liberates the individual not only from private seclusion and from the excessive claims of the social system but also from the narrow parochialism of one's own church body. It is the Lord's supper, not a church's supper. Certainly, the liberation that can be found here is a spiritual one, rooted in the symbolism of the sacramental act of eucharistic communion, quite as the community of the participants is primarily a spiritual and symbolic one. But the more the symbolism as such becomes effective in human life, the more the symbolic meaning of the eucharistic liturgy and communion will be understood and meditated. It may profoundly transform one's attitudes to other people, to society, to one's own church, and to the task of Christian unity.

At the beginning of our discussion we noted that human society and the sense of community feed to a large extent on the symbols that embody their reality. This is particularly true of the church as a symbolic community whose reason for existence is to be a symbol. Thus the symbolic form of the eucharistic community is not an argument against its potential effectiveness. On the contrary, it conditions the manifestation of the spirit of freedom and joy that the eucharistic liturgy should convey. In order to allow this cheerful spirit to manifest itself, finally, the element of play that is involved in a symbolic presentation and performance should not be suppressed. The playful exuberance of the eucharistic liturgy tenderly intimates the spiritual freedom it promises. This is often obscured by the advocates of liturgical renewal themselves, in the development of legalisms in observing liturgical form. Certainly, every game must follow its rules, and thus the discipline of liturgical behavior need not quench the spirit of Christian freedom. But the symbol is understood as symbol only if it is not mistaken for the thing itself. Only if liturgical legalism is avoided can the symbolism of the Eucharist be fully effective in producing and nourishing that sense of freedom which is the glory of a Christian life.

III
Sanctification
and Politics

ONLY DECADES ago, the assumption that Christianity and politics should be kept separate was widespread in many Christian churches. More recently, however, such aloofness has come under attack as a self-deceptive privatization of the Christian faith, self-deceptive because it disregards the inevitably political implications of any position taken in the context of social life. No important factor in social life can completely avoid involvement in political controversy, since silence adds to the strength of the prevailing position. The recognition of this inevitability has been the major contribution of what was called in the 1960s "political theology," associated specifically with the name of Johann Baptist Metz. Beyond such awareness, however, particular forms of political commitment have been promoted in the name of Christian faith. In the Calvinistic tradition, especially in America, the idea of civil freedom and, therefore, of some affinity to republican institutions (if not to democratic ones) was considered a direct implication of the Christian idea of freedom. In many countries, nationalism was accepted as a matter of natural loyalty of the Christian citizen. This happened in predominantly Lutheran countries as well and was connected, then, with the obligation to obey civil authority. Thus the Christian faith was often involved in some specific form of political commitment. Nevertheless, there are some things quite new in recent political theology. The first is the *element of contrast and opposition* to the present culture and form of society. This negative attitude to the present system of society was primarily associated with the new emphasis on eschatology. It was presaged already by Karl Barth, who in the early 1920s stressed the negative relation of eschatology to the present world in terms of the divine judgment on the world. Later on, his ethics of Christ's Kingship tried to develop a more positive correspondence between Christology and what is and should be done in the world. Remarkably enough, though, it was not so much this latter idea but rather his earlier emphasis on eschatology that was later recovered by the "theology of hope" in the work of Jürgen Moltmann. The theology of hope continued the basically negative attitude toward the present world. The primary modification consisted in changing the opposing principle from the eternal word of God to the divine promise of a future kingdom of peace and justice to come.

It is important to keep in mind that negating the present state of society is the basis for this modern political theology. In the course of history, the development of negative attitudes toward given forms of social life has never been unusual, but in the contemporary situation this did not arise from some positive principle—like religious liberty—which was missing from the structures of political life. Rather, it was the negative attitude of dialectical theology over against the natural world that tended to deny the present society whatever elements of peace and justice it might incorporate, in order to confront it with the ideal of the eschatological future.

Secondly, this eschatological dualism was associated with a call not only to relativize but also to transform the present world according to the eschatological kingdom. Because of the negative character of the basic eschatological perspective, however, it became difficult to relate the resulting urge for transformation to the intrinsic problems of the present culture. It is at this point that, in the third place, the eschatological dualism arising from dialectical theology could easily be combined with Marxist socialism. While the future of the eschatological kingdom is understood to produce the most radical revolution, the revolutions of the proletariat and of other allegedly oppressed sections of society and of the human world in general are likely candidates for the concrete manifestation of the eschatological revolution. After all, did not the God of the Bible always favor the oppressed over their oppressors, and has he not been pressing their liberation continually since the exodus?

Karl Barth, in the days of his commentary on Paul's letter to the Romans, insisted on the divine judgment as extending over *all* human efforts *alike*, revolutionary or conservative.[12] Later, however, in his famous lecture on Christian and civil community, he reverted to his earlier preferences for a socialist society[13] on the basis of a presumed analogy to God's care for the poor and forsaken. The negativity of the eschatological crisis and judgment was mollified by the principle of analogy. He was not disturbed by the ambiguities lurking beneath such apparent analogies, and such striking unawareness of them may have been due to Barth's general neglect of natural and experiential evidence in theological argument. This was a lasting effect of his negative conception of eschatology in relation to the existing world of human society. The same direction has been evident in Moltmann, who saw an affinity between the eschatological mission of Christianity and revolutionary and even chiliastic movements in modern history, emphasizing the "socialization of mankind" as one aspect of salvation in addition to justice, humanization, and universal peace.[14]

While in 1964 this was expressed in rather modest form, by 1967 Moltmann recognized Marxist socialism as the most recent, if incomplete, phase in the revolutionary process of human liberation. And in 1972 his "political theology of the cross" characterized socialism as the "symbol of human liberation from the magic cycle of poverty."[15] If the "liberation theologians" appropriated the new eschatology of the "theology of hope" on the basis of a more emphatically political alignment with a Marxist critique of the capitalist society and together with a commitment to a Marxist type of revolutionary movement of "liberation," they did so in significant continuity with the theology of hope, even if they increasingly tend to discount that relationship in their general dismissal of "European" theology. In fact, the strictly eschatological emphasis faded from liberation theology in favor of a more developmental and inductive attitude toward evaluating social realities. Still, theological interpretations of the social process in terms of a divine history of liberation from oppressive powers draw for their Christian legitimation on more recent forms of the eschatological reconstruction of political theology.

The development that we have briefly traced evolved within ongoing theological discussion. It was not of itself a development in spirituality. The influence of this theological development in various parts of the world may be due, not primarily to theological reflection on the content of the Christian tradition, but to the fact that it expresses a concern that is basically a spiritual one. Gustavo Gutiérrez spoke of a *spirituality* of liberation as of a spiritual experience that implies a restructuring of Christian life according to contemporary needs, i.e., a commitment to the liberation of people from oppression and exploitation. The center of this spirituality, according to Gutiérrez, is a conversion *to* oppressed people, to the exploited social classes, to a race treated contemptibly, and to dependent and dominated

countries.[16] Here, the basic concern of what may be called a
spirituality of liberation is phrased in a language reminiscent
of a long-standing tradition of biblical and Christian parti-
sanship for those who suffer poverty and injustice. Nevertheless, the program of social revolution that the "theology
of liberation" seeks to legitimate by calling upon attitudes
dear to every authentic Christian is significantly different
from the consequences derived from them by the Christian
church in earlier periods of Christian history. The main
tradition this revolutionary spirituality of liberation calls
upon is that of millenarianism, which in the past, at least in
some of its forms, produced similar visions of revolutionary
change in the social system.[17]

The importance of this new millenarianism of political
liberation, however, would be underestimated if it were
considered a random phenomenon in contemporary Christianity, as medieval millenarianism is usually regarded in
relation to the medieval church. For one thing, in contemporary Christianity no single ecclesial institution embodies the
tremendous solidity of the medieval church. Secondly, in
the contemporary world there exists a secular millenarianism, Marxist socialism, that recommends itself as a natural
ally to the modern Christian millenarian, although it is
possible to raise questions as to the natural or unnatural
character of this alliance between religious and secular
chiliasm. Finally, however, there is a good chance for this
new millenarianism of political liberation to carry considerable segments of so-called mainstream Christianity. This
reflects the fact that the hold of the Christian faith on the
social reality of human experience is dwindling. In addition,
in the Protestant world there is a degree of affinity (although
by no means identity) between political millenarianism and
the Calvinistic tradition, especially in that development of
the Calvinistic spirituality called "neo-Calvinism" by Ernst
Troeltsch.[18] This affinity seems to lend Christian plausibility

to the commitment of many Christians to Marxist millenari-anism. It seems remarkable that the new millenarianism of political liberation arose in such close contact with modern Calvinistic theology as represented by Barth and Moltmann. One should certainly regard it as inappropriate to deal with contemporary theological positions simply by tracing them back to denominational sources, because such a strategy cannot do justice to them either as contemporary phenome-na or as truth claims. Still, denominational mentalities undeniably influence the way theologians look at contempo-rary issues, and self-critical awareness requires us to take into account the subcutaneous influence of our denomina-tional heritage by continually revising both our own denomi-national tradition and our view of others in order to over-come the impasse between traditional positions.

Thus, in examining the affinity as well as the distinction between "neo-Calvinism" and political millenarianism, I am not pleading for some sort of Lutheran "two kingdom" doctrine. The weaknesses of this doctrine seem more obvi-ous than many Lutheran theologians, especially in Germa-ny, would be willing to admit even today. It is not enough to pity those who commit themselves to a secular millenarian-ism. Modern tendencies to draw direct conclusions from central ideas of the Christian faith to ways of dealing with the structures of social life are to be taken more seriously than is possible on the basis of the traditional Lutheran doctrine. It is not enough to pity those who commit them-selves to a secular millenarianism. Such an attitude may be quite appropriate, because the religious concern in such commitment will inevitably encounter tragic disappoint-ment. But pity is not enough and neither is mere rejection, because there is also an element of truth in the identification of religion with politics. The Augustinian and Lutheran differentiation between the two kingdoms never did justice to the element of truth in political piety. Thus, the most important contributions to the modern development of a Christian political ethics came from Calvinism and from the Baptist tradition rather than directly from the Lutheran Reformation. It seems necessary to incorporate the achievements of Calvinistic and Baptist ideas concerning civil liberty in any contemporary theological synthesis of political ethics, whereas the Lutheran separation of the spiritual from the secular kingdom may contribute not more than a cautioning note concerning the difference between the ultimate reality of the kingdom of God, which the church is primarily concerned with, and the provisional character of every institutional form, that of the secular state as well as the organization of the church.[19] While this difference between the ultimate and the provisional should not be glossed over lest one arrive at idolatrous and self-delusive conclusions, there still remains the necessary question of how provisional models and solutions for restructuring the social system of human life in secular society as well as in the church can be derived from the center of the Christian faith. On this question the Calvinist tradition has been far more effective in Protestant history.

An important difference of Calvin's theology from the earlier forms of Lutheran doctrine has often been found in his emphasis on sanctification. There is no ambiguity in Luther's assumption that genuine faith will produce good works as the good tree will bring forth good fruits. Occasionally, Luther could even speak of a progress to be made by the Christian in the mortification of the flesh, and he considered the law to be helpful in this struggle against the flesh.[20] But Calvin systematized these ideas in a new way by describing penitence as a process of regeneration or "conversion" (*Institutes* III.3.5) taking place in the individual. Luther, on the other hand, considered penitence identical with faith, the individual being placed outside himself or herself by the act of faith. At this point, Calvin's psychological interpretation of penitence as a process taking place in the individual was closer to medieval scholasticism and especially to Melanchthon than to Luther, although it was Luther's doctrine on justification which he restated in this way. The event of this transformation of our souls entails, in Calvin's view, our justification as well as our sanctification (*Institutes* III.3.6f. and 11.1ff.). Justification and sanctification form an inseparable unity, both indicating that Christ through his Spirit is dwelling in us.[21] Calvin's understanding of conversion as a process that takes place inside the individual also explains his controversial statements about one's own experience of sanctification as a sign of being elected,[22] his encouragement of self-examination. Further, the interpretation of justification and sanctification as elements in the process of conversion explains Calvin's high esteem for moral discipline in the church.[23] Since by the spirit the Christian is inserted into Christ, it is the body of Christ he or she is inserted into, and since this happens in the process of individual conversion, it is only natural that the members of the body care not only for themselves but also for each other. Although the activism of sanctification takes place primarily in the individual, it is also a communal concern.

The question may be asked here of how regeneration and sanctification are related to the political community. It is a question that was not explicitly discussed in Calvin's writings, because he clearly distinguished between the sanctifying activity of the divine spirit in the church and the secular realm of civil government. Even within the church, sanctification is primarily a process of regeneration in the individual, not in the community. Nevertheless, there are, in Calvin's view, points of correspondence between the two realms. First, secular government is not only the expression of a general divine concern for the preservation of human society but also a function and ministry that needs charismatic endowment by the Spirit of God.[24] This is not, of course, the regenerating and salvific activity of the Spirit, which is limited to the church, but an extension of the Spirit's work in all creation. Yet it is the same Spirit who is fully revealed to the faithful. Further, all secular government exhibits an image of the kingdom of Christ, the eternal King. Although only the church is the spiritual kingdom of Christ,[25] all secular administrators are summoned to submit themselves humbly to the great king Jesus Christ and to his spiritual scepter.[26] Secular administrators, therefore, are expected to observe and execute not only the commandments of the second table of the Decalogue but also those of the first. They must promote, preserve, and defend the true religion,[27] and the legitimacy of their power depends on their obedience concerning the provisions of the divine law. Thus, although Calvin distinguished between the secular society and the spiritual kingdom of Christ in the church, there is a closer connection between the two in his view than, say, in Luther's doctrine of the two kingdoms, a closer relation also than in the Augustinian tradition in general. It is the influence of the theocratic thrust of the Old Testament on Calvin's theology that most readily explains this peculiar tendency in his thought.[28]

The authority of the Old Testament in Calvin's thought also sheds light on his convictions concerning the ideal form of civil government. Like the Deuteronomist who commented on the rise of monarchy in ancient Israel (e.g., I Samuel 8), Calvin was deeply suspicious of monarchical government, especially of hereditary monarchy. As he explicitly said, such monarchies are not reconcilable with the political freedom that civil government should promote.[29] His preference for a republican, though aristocratic, form of government was determined not only by his humanistic perspective but also by his understanding of the Scriptures. He considered the charismatic leadership of Moses and of the time of the Judges to be a divine example of the ideal form of civil government, an opinion that fits very well in his general "pneumatocratic" outlook.[30] Thus there is a significant correspondence between the process of sanctification in the individual Christian and the conception of civil government. Although the two remain distinct, both are subordinated to the activity and purposes of the divine Spirit. Thus it must seem natural that Christians will commit themselves to the purposes of the divine Spirit in the realm of civil government too.

The famous theory of Max Weber held that Calvinist piety was at the roots of modern capitalism because individual Christians in the process of their sanctification were expected to develop a rationally calculated and disciplined life, an ascetic life-style rooted in their sense of vocation and prompted by the desire to reassure themselves of their vocation and election by success in their endeavors toward sanctification. With this argument, Weber was able to show the great impact of a religious motivation on the formation of the modern economy. But his description was one-sided because he limited his study to the economic behavior of Calvinists. He deliberately separated this private aspect of Puritan ethics from the Puritan social commitment, which aimed not only at the Christian community but also at a theocratic reconstruction of the entire political order. This point has been made repeatedly since Ernst Troeltsch, and also in recent years by the controversial work of Michael Walzer and in a more balanced way by James L. Adams: Puritan efforts at sanctification entailed also communal and political consequences. It has been an important element of the strength of Calvinist spirituality that it involves a tendency to political reconstruction of the social system. The secular realm is not considered a separate reality where Christian principles do not apply, nor are there only the general principles of natural law that the church expects human government to observe. Rather, there is a specifically Christian conception of theocracy that serves as a criterion in evaluating the achievements of administrative politics as well as the political form of the social system in general. And yet this attitude differs from millenarianism because it does not claim to realize the eschatological kingdom of Christ in this world by means of political action. The difference between the church and the world, between sanctification and politics, is preserved in principle. In modern presentations of Calvinistic political ethics, as in Karl Barth's view, that difference is expressed by speaking of a mere *analogy* of secular society to the Christian community. There is a latent danger, however, that these distinctions will be blurred by the dynamics of the theocratic principle.

This danger was acutely felt in the course of the Puritan revolution in England, when the Presbyterians tried to impose their own form of religious uniformity on the entire country. A significant breakthrough in the history of Christian political thought occurred when, confronted by the demand for Presbyterian uniformity, the English Independents adopted the principle of religious freedom. This was not seen as a compromise and surrender of Puritan principles but rather as the completion and consequence of the idea of Christian freedom, the "reform of the Reformation itself," as Milton and others saw it.[31] Indeed, the correspondence between Christian and civil liberty could be taken from the writings of Calvin himself. The one factor that had to be added was the doctrine of the original sovereignty of the people, a doctrine that Calvin had not accepted.[32] Certainly, religious pluralism entailed a break with the ideal of theocratic uniformity that one could derive from Calvin, but it did not mean the surrender of the theocratic ideal as such. On the contrary, Milton celebrated the English liberty as having established the principle that God alone is sovereign. And Cromwell, in an important address to Parliament in 1657, speaking of religious and civil liberty as "the two greatest concernments that God hath in the world," described religion as God's peculiar interest which intends both that all its professors enjoy "due and just liberty" and that they use that liberty "to assert the truth of God."[33] Thus, religious as well as political freedom could be seen as manifesting the sovereignty of God, while the false theocracy of dogmatic uniformity was eliminated.

This "neo-Calvinist" model (as Troeltsch called it) for relating religion and society was clearly understood as a political realization of the principle of Christian freedom, the basic principle of the Reformation. Nevertheless, this was not a chiliastic model, because it was based on a fundamental opposition between God, who alone rules, and his creatures, none of whom is entitled to exercise monarchical rule or to claim the divine truth exclusively. The principle of pluralism in politics as well as in religion indicates that neither any man nor any woman is God. This message is clear enough, but it also reveals an ambiguity inherent in the Christian legitimation of religious and civil liberty. Christian freedom as conceived by the apostle Paul and John the Evangelist, and as recovered in the Reformation doctrine of justification by faith alone, expresses the unity of the believer with God through Christ, while modern principles of religious and civil liberty function on the basis of the difference between God's kingdom and human government, between divine truth and the human teaching of that divine truth. How, then, can that religious and civil liberty be considered a consequence of the freedom of the Christian in community with God by faith? Is there only a delusive ambiguity in the use of the same term ("freedom," or "liberty") in both cases? The apparent analogy may indeed be misleading. Arbitrary choice and the Christian idea of freedom through communion with God have little in common. If in the case of Calvin, as in the Puritan revolution, the analogy between Christian and political freedom is not only due to the equivocal nature of language, it is because the meaning of political and religious freedom was seen in the immediacy of human individuals to God under the guidance of the divine Spirit. In contrast to subordination to human rule, political freedom is freedom to the degree that the individual will be ruled by the spirit of God. And religious freedom from obedience to human authorities is freedom only insofar as it provides the possibility of professing the truth of God. Otherwise it is only license for individual arbitrariness. Now it may be necessary to accept the risk that freedom may be perverted into mere license in order to keep open the possibility of authentic freedom. But the political principles of civil and religious freedom do not tell by themselves whether they will be used one way or the other. A basic ambiguity, therefore, remains in the concept of freedom concerning the relation of civil and religious freedom in the Protestant teaching of the freedom of the Christian.

In the perspective of a theological evaluation, this ambiguity became more critical when liberalism later defined the principle of freedom on the basis of natural law alone.[34] The liberal conception of freedom came close, as an ideology, to a chiliastic model of social life. But it was a secular form of chiliasm, since it now surrendered the idea of theocracy. This secular chiliasm (or millenarianism) resulted from the fact that the confrontation and correspondence between Christian community and secular society ceased to function as an element of political theory. Consequently, the theocratic conception disappeared, to be replaced by the secular chiliasm of the liberal ideology that now functioned as a *civil* religion. In this phase of the development, then, the analogy between Christian and civil liberty began to conceal the opposition between liberalism as a political ideology (or a civil religion) and the Christian theocratic ideal. Without the theocratic element, that analogy could mean the surrender of the Christian faith to a secular triumphalism. The delusive character of the ideology of liberalism was pointed out by Reinhold Niebuhr[35] and earlier by Karl Marx in his critique of the merely formal character of bourgeois liberties. The truth of such criticism notwithstanding, the negative element in the modern principles of religious and civil liberty remains valid: They effectively deny any human doctrine and any human government the absolute authority that can be claimed by God alone. In this negative assumption the liberal culture continued to be silently dependent on the theocratic idea.

It is precisely at this point that the contemporary "theology of liberation" breaks with the liberal tradition. It does not offer any means to prevent tyrannical rule by an elite that might obtain power under the pretext of "liberating" the people from oppression, as was usually the case in revolutionary coups or wars. Some liberation theologians are so unaware of the dangers at this point that they even reject the distinction in European eschatological theology between the ultimate future of God's kingdom and the provisional and fragmentary anticipations of that future in human action.[36] They are afraid it might erode the confidence of people in committing themselves to a model of social change if they are kept from believing that they are fighting for absolute truth. Strangely enough, the liberation theologians do not seem to fear the idolatrous fanaticism of revolutionaries who believe their opponents to be enemies of the absolute truth itself.

The underlying problem that the Barthian and the eschatological forms of political theology have in common with liberation theology is the ambiguity of their language about liberation and oppression. Barth derived the principle of civil liberty from the liberty of the children of God by analogy. This had been done by the English Independents of the seventeenth century, but in their case, as in the case of Calvin, it did not provide their only argument. In the case of Calvin it was his humanistic preference for the premonarchical form of government in ancient Israel (as in Rome) in connection with his pneumatocratic and theocratic ideas. In the case of the Independents it was the idea of the sovereignty of the people and the implied principles of natural law, together with the thoroughgoing distinction between divine and human authority and, in addition, the continuing influence of the pneumatocratic ideal. Barth, of course, shared the concern for the distinction between divine and human authority. But this led him to preclude any argument from human experience and reason, and thus he was left with the ambiguities of analogical reasoning from Christological assertions. The theocratic element, outside the walls of the church, became an empty assertion of the theologian. Since the "theology of hope" in a similar way confronts the secular world with the prophetic promise of the Bible, it also tends to identify similarities of language as analogies (or anticipations) of the prophetic promise without establishing empirically to what degree the phenomena are comparable to what the prophetic promise had in mind. This rather careless way of establishing relations of theological language to historical and contemporary phenomena is understandable if one remembers that these theologies started by confronting the world with the Word of God without systematically attributing theological significance to the experience, history, and self-understanding of that world.

A further example of this procedure, but also a new problem, occurs in liberation theology. Gustavo Gutiérrez distinguishes three levels of liberation: a political and economic one, another of human self-emancipation in history, and, finally, the biblical one.[37] He assumes without further discussion that all these conceptions of liberation complement each other, and he explicitly says they are mutually inclusive, representing only different "levels" of a single process of liberation. But what if these different phenomena have little more in common than the word "liberation"? What if the conception of human history as a process of human self-liberation emerged in diametrical opposition to the Christian affirmation that human beings become free, not by themselves, but only by the spirit of Christ? How is it possible to harmonize such a conflict by speaking of "levels" in one and the same process? But Gutiérrez does not try to harmonize, he merely overlooks the problem. And he does very little to defend his assertion that there is more than merely a verbal relation between the Christian message of liberation from the power of sin by Jesus Christ and "the aspirations of social classes and oppressed nations" for their liberation. The problem is that the aspirations of social classes and of nations who think of themselves as oppressed are not necessarily justified. Whether they are or whether their claims are excessive can be determined only by standards of justice. Only a theory of justice can establish that inequalities among individuals are inescapable and determine which of these inequalities are justified (or at least tolerable) on the basis of different individual contributions to the social system. John Rawls's *A Theory of Justice*[38] and the discussion aroused by that book demonstrate the difficulties of such a theory. The basic problem in this discussion seems to lie in the question whether such a theory should start with the assumption of the traditional social contract theory, the assumption of an "original position" of isolated and equal individuals, or whether such abstractions are to be considered misleading, in which case the concept of justice must be developed in connection with a description of the social system and the hierarchy of its values. I prefer the second alternative and regard a particular concept of society, structured by a hierarchy of values to

be realized through that system, as theoretically indispensable for any concrete application of the Aristotelian *suum
cuique,* the notion of distributive justice. But however a
concept of justice may be established, it is only on the basis
of such a concept that aspirations of particular individuals
or groups can be qualified, whether justified or excessive.
Gutiérrez has no interest in such a criterion of justice but
simply refers to the aspirations of classes and oppressed
nations. But again, whether a group or nation is actually
"oppressed" is to be determined only by reference to
standards of justice.[39] If they are not justified by a standard
of justice, cries and complaints about "oppression" may be
excessive, and if they express excessive self-affirmation,
they may have less in common with liberation from the
power of sin by Jesus Christ than with sin itself. How, then,
is such a tendency to self-affirmation against every social
limitation to be regarded as just another "level" of the
process of liberation from self-centeredness that occurs by
the Spirit of God, which alone, according to the Scriptures,
produces true freedom?

It is not by accident, of course, that Gutiérrez and other
liberation theologians avoid head-on discussion of the concept of justice. After the breakdown of the equation of
revealed law with the Christian theory of "relative" natural
law there is no generally accepted Christian theory of justice
today. It does not help to invoke the Christian idea of love in
its place. Certainly, the concept of love is the most basic
Christian criterion even of justice, but it is only in connection with a concept of justice that love is concrete in a social
situation. Without an idea of justice, it makes little sense to
talk about "orthopraxis" as a criterion of faith instead of
doctrine. The outcry for "orthopraxis" may primarily indicate today the uneasy awareness that a criterion of justice is
lacking.

This problem also occurs in some forms of black theology

that may be considered special forms of liberation theology. While South African black theologians such as Manas Buthelezi[40] use the label "black theology" in relation to the task of interpreting the reality of black humanity in terms of its divine destiny, James Cone relates black theology to a program of revolutionary political "liberation" of black people.[41] In his view, God seems to be exclusively their God since they are the oppressed ones. The self-interest of the black people and the will of God are identified. Cone's views often come uncomfortably close to a black racism which he certainly does not intend. In order to avoid that danger, he would have to deal with God's affirmation of the life of black *and* white human beings and with their common calling in the one church out of all nations and races. This would not preclude the concern for a special calling of black people today, but within the framework of the universal church and not in terms of hostility against others. Cone might claim that such hostility would refer to white people only in their function as oppressors. But at this point, again, a general theory of justice applying to all races is necessary in order to establish what should be called "oppression."

In this situation, liberation theology replaces ethics with social theory. This can be done, however, only because Marxism, the social theory selected by the liberation theologians for a normative role in their thought, includes ethical elements—elements of the "absolute" form of natural law[42]—and because the entire Marxist analysis of capitalist society can be read as an explanation for why in bourgeois society natural law is prevented from functioning as it should according to liberalism. At the same time, the Marxist theory points out how a situation will be created which allows for the proper functioning of liberty and equality, the basic principles of natural law. Because Marxism, if only by means of social revolution, holds such a situation to be attainable, it is a chiliastic system, a secular millenarianism. This is why, in liberation theology, Marxism could replace an ethical theory of justice. There is, however, no critical reflection in liberation theology concerning the reconcilability of Marxist economic theory, especially its concept of class conflict, with the Christian faith. Nor is there a critical investigation of the empirical reliability of the theoretical framework of the Marxist analysis of capitalist society. The Marxist theory of value, derived exclusively from human labor as well as from the key notion of "surplus value," has met with devastating criticism. But without the concept of surplus value there is no theoretical basis for the notions of exploitation and alienation in the Marxist sense of those terms. Consequently, if a Marxist speaks of oppression, one must be careful regarding the empirical evidence and theoretical interpretation such language is based upon. If liberation theologians were not committed Marxists, their diagnosis of "oppression" in their societies might be far more credible than it is now, considering its weak theoretical basis. But by asking for a commitment in the class conflict, as Gutiérrez does, they require also a commitment to Marxist analysis prior to theological reflection, as Juan Luis Segundo explicitly states in his recent book *The Liberation of Theology*. The call for commitment prior to critical reflection sounds familiar, and if we reject such a demand in relation to the traditional Christian message, we have a right to reject it in the case of the Marxist commitment of the liberation theologians as well. In the case of liberation theology, we have an extreme example of a political theology, the argument of which proceeds only by vague analogies from Christian soteriological language. This renders Christian language (and faith) subservient to another concern that is not open to question. The vagueness of such analogies may conceal the danger of shifting loyalties for those who engage in this kind of theology.

The spirituality involved here seems to start from disenchantment with the present social system. This disenchantment is nourished from many sources. One source, especially important for dialectical theology, has been the effect of World War I on optimism concerning Western culture. Another very general one is certainly the meaninglessness of the bureaucratic system in modern industrialized society (Peter Berger). A more specific source is poverty in some so-called developing countries. But since problems of poverty and human suffering have existed throughout the centuries, this last experience alone cannot explain the rise of the new political spirituality. It must be seen also as a reaction to the criticism of religion as a narcotic contributing to the persistence of otherwise intolerable political structures. In many cases there is also a feeling that traditional religion is irrelevant and that it might be made relevant again by translating it into politics. All these factors, and others, may contribute to the astonishing fascination of Marxism even for contemporary theology. This is astonishing not only because the Marxist theoretical scheme ought to be intellectually discredited by now in its most fundamental points, but also because there is broad evidence in the historical experience of this century for the suspicion that the social theory upon which "liberation theologians" rely for their hope of liberation will finally lead to an even more systematically oppressive system than the one they now combat.

In order to cope with the mood of raising political positions to the status of religious commitments, Christian theology should strengthen the connection between sanctification and politics. This must not be conceived, however, as a sequence of vague analogies that may lead to the actual, if unintended, surrender of that faith itself. Some of its necessary threads are the following.

First, the theocratic element is indispensable. This must be renewed on the basis of a pluralistic, "ecumenical" spirituality, leaving behind the older problem of dogmatic uniformity. Without a new expression of the theocratic idea, sanctification cannot be extended to the religous substructures of society. We may expect such a new manifestation of the theocratic idea as a possible by-product of the ecumenical process of Christian reunification.

Second, the step from sanctification to politics cannot be successful without a Christian theory of social justice. Such a theory would have to work out a critical description of the social system and its institutions in the context of its religious presuppositions, which, in the Christian tradition, are always rooted in history. In other words, the contractual element must be restated in the context of a covenantal definition of the particular societies (Richard Neuhaus).

The political impact of a Christian theory of justice will depend upon the renewal of the theocratic idea; and a spiritual theocracy can be effective only through a theory of justice that uses the theocratic framework in redefining social reality. Without those two elements it is hard to see how a "political theology" can be saved from the temptation to render the gospel subservient to concerns other than the glory of the God who revealed himself in Jesus Christ.

IV
The Absence of God
in Theological Perspective

1

SINCE the time of the literary figure Jean Paul (1763–1825) and the philosopher G. W. F. Hegel (1770–1831), people have talked about the absence or death of God as a feature of the modern secular world. Despite important differences however, between absence and death, these two symbols shall be treated here as functionally equivalent in describing the character of modern culture. Such a description is intended when either the absence or the death of God is talked about. It is not itself an expression of the religious consciousness, although the phenomenon pointed to by those symbols certainly concerns religious persons living in the modern world. What is at stake here is not a metaphysical thesis about the reality of God but an experiential phenomenon in cultural history. Talk about the death or the absence of God points to the fact that the interpretation of the world, as well as the behavior of human beings in the everyday life of modern culture, gets along without reference to God. This is true of modern life as it is represented by the public media, but it also applies to the private lives of most people, even of Christians themselves in the ordinary situations of their life in a secular culture. The fact that the

Christian churches, together with a rather lively religious concern, continue to exist in the midst of such a culture is easily taken as a matter of only secondary importance. It does not seem to make much difference whether one takes them for dying relics of the past or as compensating for certain shortcomings of secular culture. This cultural phenomenon has implications, of course, for the metaphysical question of the reality of God, and its impact shapes religious consciousness as it tries to resist that cultural trend. Thus it is not surprising that it also affects theological reflection, which is generally more open to changing sensitivities of the cultural scene.

The metaphysical conclusions derived from the cultural diagnosis will differ according to whether one speaks of the absence of God or the death of God. The latter phrase usually implies that the ungodliness of the modern secular world has effected a definitive, epochal, and irreversible change in the direction of cultural evolution. In comparison, Hegel's use of the phrase "death of God" to imply a possible resurrection of God in the human spirit may be one of the authentic roots of that description of the modern situation, but it remains hopelessly esoteric. To most people, the death of God in modern culture stands for a definitive event. When the same cultural phenomenon is described not as the death of God but as evidence for the absence of God in modern culture, we express a certain measure of reserve about drawing metaphysical conclusions from cultural situations or we even attempt to conceive the reality of God in the face of the ungodliness of modern secular culture, though as absent from that cultural world. It seems important, however, to relativize the difference and opposition of these metaphysical interpretations by relating all of them to their common basis in the diagnosis of culture. Whether one talks of the death of God or simply of the absence of God, both cases refer to the atheism of modern secular culture. To that extent, the two phrases are functionally equivalent, though not perhaps equally appropriate. On the contrary, reducing talk about the absence or death of God to its function in describing the modern cultural situation makes it possible to compare both descriptions and to judge their respective appropriateness.

2

Several factors make up the phenomenon underlying the description of modern culture in terms of the death of God or the absence of God. In the first place, the world of secular culture is shaped by modern science, which explains the world of nature without the hypothesis of God's existence. But even more momentous than this theoretical achievement is its application in modern technology. Armed with a technology based on scientific description of natural processes, modern society transforms its world in such a way that the praxis of human life with its risks and contingencies is brought under extensive human control. In this context, interference by God would only be a disturbance.

The development of modern technological society has changed the character of social life. With the rise of industrialization and bureaucratic organization in modern society the life of the individual has become increasingly dependent on systems of social organization that derive their sense of justification from their function of organizing the common effort at cultivating and exploiting the resources of the natural world. In the framework of this system of social organization the individual inevitably feels powerless and manipulated by anonymous forces, the personalizations of which in capitalists, functionaries, politicians, and bureaucrats are often shadowy and mutually interchangeable. On the other hand, the dependence of human life on the contingencies of nature and history has

been so drastically-reduced by modern medicine and insur-
ance systems, by rational organization of economic processes as well as of political change, that individuals seem less
vulnerable to the vagaries of fortune. At least in the world of
everyday life the precariousness of human existence has
been suppressed to a large extent and with increasing
success. The significance of these consequences of the
technological and bureaucratic organization of modern society in relation to the practical atheism of modern individual
life has been correctly emphasized by Dorothee Soelle.[43]
Jesus' word against excessive caring (Matt. 6:25ff.) was
perhaps always taken as a paradox, since the human awareness of a future different from the present inevitably entails
the need for self-preservation and for making provision for
future contingencies. But never in history were those provisions developed into such a comprehensive and successful
system of collective security. It is now a patent observation
that people tend to forget God when they are physically
well-to-do. In this sense the atheism of modern secular
culture confirms the tension between caring and faith in God
that was highlighted by Jesus.

There are three factors, then, that condition the secularity
of modern culture: modern science, technology, and the
increasing social organization and control that produce a
comparatively high measure of security in individual life. A
fourth factor is sometimes added: the anthropocentric structure of modern culture. In modern Western culture, the
human person is no longer the image and representative of
God, but rather the substitute for God. Modern humanity
expelled God from creation in assuming the function of
divine providence and taking up the burden of responsibility
for the social and even for the natural order of the world.
Certainly it was the biblical tradition itself that assigned to
humanity the function of representing the rule of God in the
world of creation. This was the meaning of the distinctive-

ness of the human creature as image of God, but that position of dignity also meant human stewardship over God's creation rather than its domination and exploitation for arbitrary human purposes. The notion of humanity as created in the image of God documents the belief that anthropocentrism need not be antichristian or atheist. But the anthropocentric thrust of modern secular culture did indeed develop in a process of emancipation from the God of the Christian faith. This tendency of modernity was articulated by such men as the young William Blake (1757–1827) and Friedrich Nietzsche (1844–1900). Their interpretation of human freedom as emancipation from all authority and especially from the religious authority of the Christian tradition is paradigmatic of the atheism of modern culture. Certainly, for a long time leading figures of modern culture expressed their thought only rarely in explicitly atheistic form, and this is still exceptional in the Western cultural context. But implicitly, everyday life in modern society as shaped by modern science and technology is everywhere atheistic. Insofar as institutional life has no place for God, within the context of that world individuals behave as if there were none. By all practical standards this counts as a substantially atheistic attitude, the positive correlation of which consists in an anthropocentrism constituted by emancipation from the religious tradition of Christianity and by a determination to consider no longer God but humanity itself the ultimate criterion. The consequence of this brand of anthropocentrism proclaimed by Nietzsche and amply confirmed during the century following his prophecy of nihilism, has been the devaluation of all formerly normative human values. When moral and legal norms, and even aesthetic and theoretical ones as well, are seen as imposed by human authorities, they inevitably lose their power, and the social world dissolves into the utilitarian strategies of its individual components.

In 1957 Gabriel Vahanian used the phrase "the death of God" for his analysis of contemporary culture and became the father of the short-lived fad of a "theology" of the death of God. Although he offered as critical analysis what others were to make a program, he presented the anthropocentric mentality of secular humanity, a creature of modern science and technology, in contrast to theocentric Christianity as the decisive character of the phenomenon of God's absence or "death" in modern culture. According to Vahanian, the contemporary anthropocentric attitude "expresses . . . the irrelevance of God . . . to concrete existence."[44] Vahanian's analysis was deeply influenced by the theology of Karl Barth. Certainly Barth in his volume on the modern history of Protestant theology had not used the phrase "death of God" to describe the culture of enlightenment. To Barth, the latter-day pupil of Calvin, the reality of God and his sovereignty stood unshakable in spite of all human questioning. But in the perspective of Barth's theocentrism, the description of modern culture as anthropocentric already involved its judgment. By combining that diagnosis with the phrase "death of God" Vahanian pressed Barth's analysis to its final consequences, something that also applies to the role of modern theology in this process. According to Vahanian, Christianity—and especially modern Christian theology—contributed to the erosion of its own credibility because of its fatal tendency to appease the spirit of secular culture: "For the sake of winning the world, it lost its soul."[45] There is no way to deny that this danger accompanies all theological effort to point out the relevance of Christianity to the culture of any epoch. During the years following the publication of his book, Vahanian himself recognized the so-called theology of the death of God that developed on the basis of his cultural diagnosis as a particularly telling example of surrendering to the assumed spirit of the age.[46] His contempt was not without reason. And yet it was not simply a matter of feebly appeasing the spirit of the age that the development of modern theology has been characterized by a concentration on anthropology as basic even for the question of the truth of religion and of the Christian faith itself. In modern culture anthropology has become the basis for settling all kinds of truth questions, and if the God of the Bible really is the creator of the world, his human creature cannot fail to witness to his existence, if the evidence is assessed without prejudice. Again and again modern theology entered critically into the anthropological basis of the modern cultural consciousness, and without doing so the claim to public truth could hardly have been maintained by the Christian proclamation. It was precisely in the debate on religion and Christian faith as constitutive factors that make the human being truly human, that modern theology made its most valuable contribution to the credibility of the Christian proclamation. The fact that this has been done in the form of scholarly argument, on the basis of the modern mind informed by scientific theories and procedures, should not be judged a reprehensible adaptation of the Christian faith to the standards of human knowledge. After all, such an effort can also aim at a limitation and critical revision of rational criteria in the light of a more comprehensive awareness of reality as it characterizes Christian consciousness. It is certainly a tiresome and risky enterprise to attempt a critical transformation of the academic consciousness and of the mind of a culture. But it is through such attempts, among other things, that the struggle for the truth of a religious tradition must take place. A religious message cannot claim truth, unless it at least claims general validity. Vahanian was wrong in attributing the main responsibility for the loss of credibility of the Christian tradition in modern times to the efforts of Christian theologians to reconcile religion and science. A far greater burden of responsibility for this lies with the tenden-

cy of many forms of modern Christian piety to separate the
experience of faith from reason, as if the content of faith
were safe against critical questioning if presented in terms of
purely subjective personal conviction. In that strategy the
Christian faith inevitably presented itself as an arbitrary and
therefore irrational commitment. Time and again, Protestant pietism and revivalism emphasize the importance of
personal conviction over against the general culture. But
ironically, it was precisely this tendency that achieved an
uncritical adaptation of Christian spirituality to the anthropocentric spirit of the age. The "retreat to commitment"
(W. W. Bartley), which supposedly bases faith securely in
the citadel of private commitment, has in fact restricted
religion precisely to that corner which modern secular
culture has provided for it, the area of private conviction
without objective or public validity. To classify religion in
general and the Christian faith in particular merely as
personal conviction like other such convictions is the surest
way of subordinating them to the emancipative anthropocentrism of modern secular culture. Conceived in this way
they no longer constitute a challenge to the public spirit of
the age.

When Hegel in his famous sentence about the death of
God at the end of his essay on "faith and knowledge"
(1802–1803) called the "atheism of the moral world" the
spiritual result of the age of enlightenment, he had already
identified emancipative anthropocentrism at its root. In
philosophy Hegel saw the tendencies of that age epitomized
by the thought of J. G. Fichte (1762–1814), who places the
"absolute finitude of a subject and of its action" over
against an unreasonable world of sense perception that must
be annihilated to make room for reason. This finite subjectivity, completely turned in upon itself, is at the same time
the agency of mechanical reasoning, which in the positive
sciences takes finite entities as the only reality so that the

infinite deteriorates to an empty beyond. Thus, the idolization of the finite subject at the core of modern secular culture was not first discovered by Karl Barth and Gabriel Vahanian, but was already held responsible for the "atheism of the moral world" in Hegel's analysis of his own age. Unlike Barth, however, Hegel did not see a theology of the sovereignty of God as opposed to human subjectivity as offering the remedy for this situation. Hegel considered such opposing of the absolute to the finite to be a finitization of the absolute itself, because the very notion of the absolute would thus be constituted by its exclusion of the finite. The limitation of something by something else that at the same time constitutes its definition indicates finitude. Conceiving of the absolute reality in such a way always in fact presupposes the absoluteness of the finite subject, since according to Hegel it is impossible to conceive of anything finite except in the context of infinity. If infinity is not accepted as an absolute reality in its own right, it will be the presumed infinity of the finite subject that by implication underlies the process of its experience in perceiving finite entities. Therefore, the finitization of the concept of God by opposing it to the finite reality of creatures would be the safest way to secure the pretended infinity of the human subject itself. In Hegel's perspective, the absolutizing of finite reality can only be overcome by relativizing those oppositions. In doing so he began with the subjectivity of the finite ego, which by its self-transcending movement is already related to infinity and therefore even less separable from absolute reality than other finite entities. Thus, the finite subjectivity of the human person and the finite subjectivity of his or her knowledge were not simply rejected by Hegel in the name of the sovereignty of God but were integrated into the movement of the absolute idea of reason, and thus liberated to their authentic truth in transcending their finite reality.

While Hegel tried to conceive the reification of the finite and all the finite subjects as a momentary phase in the development of the divine idea itself, the "atheism of the moral world" turned out to be itself a necessary phase in the evolutionary process toward the realization of that "absolute freedom" which for Hegel epitomizes the principle of Christianity and especially of Protestantism. This, however, is one of the most debated points in Hegel's reconstruction of Christianity. Is it really appropriate to consider the "infinite sorrow" of a world where God is absent and finite reality, especially one's own ego, functions as absolute, in terms of a necessary passage on the way toward that freedom which—as Hegel and the Christian tradition agree—can be obtained only by communion with God?

3

According to Hegel, the absence of God in modern secular culture has been a product of Christianity itself, a product of the principle of subjective freedom which is entailed in the Christian concept of faith. While Vahanian, in emphasizing the post-Christian character of modern secular culture, holds Christianity also responsible for its emergence, he does so in a different way, not in the sense of a realization of the Christian principle in modernity, but by way of a self-surrender of Christianity in adapting itself to the secular spirit. At this point, the American "theology of the death of God" of the 1960s returned to Hegel. In 1966, William Hamilton and Thomas Altizer demanded a reinterpretation of incarnation itself as expressing the death of a transcendent God, even if this meaning of the notion of incarnation became recognizable only recently, since the nineteenth century.[47] According to Altizer, there is a liberating power in this message that will be felt as soon as one notices—as William Blake already did—that God the creator and Satan are identical. But Altizer differs from the gnosticism of Christian antiquity because he does not call upon a redeemer God against the evil creator God. Because of his version of the death of God he is able to remain a monotheist: the almighty and transcendent God annihilates himself in the act of incarnation and thereby achieves the liberation of his human creatures. This interpretation of the incarnation is closely related to the thesis of Ernst Bloch that in the incarnation the Son replaces the Father.[48] According to Bloch, Christ is "the releasing word that frees us from the Lord Father, from that robe of stars, from the fate in the highest."[49] But in contrast to Bloch, Altizer describes this loss of transcendence as an act of "kenotic" self-annihilation by God. At this point he remains a theologian, as Hegel did. Certainly, Altizer did not proclaim a resurrection of God in the spirit of the Christian community, as Hegel did. Nor is such philosophical theology of the spirit that congeals into a conceptual structure replaced, as it is for other theologians of the death of God (especially with William Hamilton), by the anticipation of a novel revelation of God in the future. In Altizer's view the death of God is not just transitory so that he could be represented by a temporary substitute, of the sort Dorothee Soelle thinks Jesus Christ to be. According to Altizer, the finality of the death of the transcendent God is the event that liberates the human creature to authentic selfhood.

All these varieties of a theology of the death of God—including that of Hegel—remain unacceptable in the perspective of a Christian theology, because they follow the model of a monophysitic (one-nature) Christology or, if one prefers, of a Sabellian (modalist) interpretation of the Trinity: The church always insisted on referring the death of Christ to his human nature. Though the significance of the incarnation and of the death of Christ to the Trinitarian life of God may not have been appropriately spelled out in

traditional Christian doctrine, that much was clearly intended: It was not the divine Logos that died on the cross, nor
was it the Father, but it was the human individual Jesus of
Nazareth. Certainly this human individual was united to the
Logos in the unity of a single person and therefore did not
remain under the power of death. But still it was the human
nature of Jesus that suffered death. These distinctions of the
orthodox Christology of the ancient church were already
blurred by Hegel when he presented the death of Jesus as
the death of God himself. Such an interpretation also
confuses the careful distinction that Jesus himself observed
between himself and his heavenly Father and that was so
characteristic of the relation of the historical Jesus to the
God whom he called his Father. That distinction became
basic in the later development of Christological and Trinitarian doctrines: It is precisely in distinguishing himself from
God, his Father, and by abstaining from any ambition to
"be like God" that Jesus of Nazareth exhibited his human
obedience to the Father and thus showed himself to be the
Son. In this behavior of Jesus is rooted the difference
between Father and Son in the Trinitarian conception of
God, as well as the Christian conviction of an irremovable
difference of the creature from God, even in the highest
forms of unity with God. Jesus' behavior in relation to his
Father shows that difference does not necessarily impede
unity. Rather, communion with God increases in the same
proportion as the modesty of the creature in distinguishing
itself from God. This also exhibits the external affirmation
by the love of God of the independent existence of the
creature. That independent existence of the creature is there
to remain, even on the level of the most intimate communion with God. Unity with God, therefore, never means the
extinction of the freedom of the creature, but rather its
inspiration and activation. Thus the divine incarnation does
not mean the absorption of what is human into the glory of

the divine light, nor does it mean the self-annihilation or death of God. The interpretation of the history of Jesus Christ as a history of the death of God is an inverted monophysitism. It not only misses the authentic form of Jesus' relation to the Father, which allowed the Father to become both manifest and present through the ministry of Jesus, but it also distorts the authentic constitution of human freedom, the specifically Christian vindication of created independence in unity with God.

The absence of God in modern secular culture, then, is not simply to be accounted for as an authentic development of Christian origins. Is it at least a "post-Christian" phenomenon that does not occur accidentally in the context of the world of Christian culture, but results from a process of erosion and dissolution of its content? This was the diagnosis of Barth and Vahanian, and while the specific form of their interpretation is not acceptable, our conclusion does not necessarily discard it altogether. It is also represented by the more recent discussion by Heinrich Döring of the "absence of God." For this Roman Catholic theologian, contemporary Protestant theology is a series of interpretations of Christianity, each of which expresses the absence of God. This applies to the absolutely transcendent God of dialectical theology as well as to the God of existential theology, who is not approachable as a being in himself, and to the God of Paul Tillich, who is absorbed into the world by disappearing into its "depth." The same phenomenon is also discernible in the God of Gerhard Ebeling, who seems to dissolve in the "word-event," and finally in the theology of hope, which seems to place God too far away in the future. For Döring all these conceptions come close to the theology of the death of God. In fact, however, they were more concerned, in their own ways, for the presence of God than Döring seems prepared to admit.

A special problem with this interpretation is the denominational perspective. Certainly there is some reason for the assumption that Protestantism, under the cultural impact of which modern secularization and ideological pluralism were first developed, must bear some responsibility for the emergence of a world without God. Hegel was the first to identify the Protestant notion of Christian freedom as the historical root of the modern liberal idea of freedom, which turned against its Christian origins in the course of the Enlightenment and came to function as a central concept in the ungodly world of modernity. But even Hegel's presentation suffers from a one-sided emphasis on history of ideas in accounting for the origins of modernity. This one-sidedness is shared by most theories on the origin of the modern world regardless of their differences in interpretation, be it conceived as realization of Christian motives as in Hegel, Gogarten, or Altizer; as resulting from a process of dissolution of the Christian faith as in Barth and Vahanian; or finally as a product of human rebellion and self-preservation against the extravagance of Christian claims for God's omnipotence as in Hans Blumenberg. Even Max Weber derived the modern world of capitalism one-sidedly from the history of Protestant ideas, i.e., from the mentality of the Calvinist confidence in one's personal election.

But no purely ideological interpretation will do justice to the relation of modernity to its Christian prehistory. Ideological constructions cannot conceal the painfully real break that separates the beginnings of the Enlightenment in the second half of the seventeenth century from the prior age of the Reformation. This break resulted from the unwanted consequences of the Reformation in more than a century of religious wars, and it is finally this reality of human suffering and social destruction that explains, as no ideological reasoning can do, the change from the Reformers' idea of freedom to its reconstruction by Locke and others in terms of natural law. The experience of the religious wars of the sixteenth and seventeenth centuries made possible the increasing acceptance of a principle of toleration founded on the neutrality of the state and of public culture over against the controversies of religion. By reducing religious confession to the status of a private conviction, its formerly public impact was replaced by a natural law that now was disengaged from its medieval Christian roots. Thus ideas of freedom and equality which were increasingly purified from their Christian connotations became the basic values of the modern secular culture that gave rise to the "atheism of the moral world."

It was not the Reformation as such, but the series of unwanted consequences, the confessional separation and the resulting catastrophe of religious wars, that provided the basis for the peculiar anthropocentrism of a modern culture characterized by the absence of God. To present this result as an effect of the Christian faith itself means to play down the seriousness of the disruption that occurred at this point in Christian cultural history. But it is also historically inappropriate to see in that result a Promethean rebellion against the Christian God. Rather, it occurred as the inevitable effect of a largely unwanted emancipation from the Christian origins of Western culture in consequence of the bracketing of confessional controversies concerning their relevance for public life, a decision that had become a matter of survival for Western societies after those controversies had exerted their destructive impact long enough. For this reason it is also inappropriate to account for the death of God in the world of modern culture as a consequence of theology's excessive desire to adapt to the anthropocentric spirit of modernity. This theory overstresses the cultural influence of theological reflection and misreads the task that presented itself to Christian theology after the epochal disruption of the religious wars. In a culture where only what was universally human could

continue to claim validity for public life, Christian theology
had inevitably to argue for the truth of the Christian faith on
that basis in order to restrain the trend to a privatization of
religious belief and to prevent the entailed erosion of the
religious consciousness of truth.

4

After clarifying the process by which the atheism of
modern secular culture arose out of the confessional antago-
nism following the Protestant Reformation, we have still to
determine its significance for a culture rooted in the Christian religion and for Christianity itself. The answer to this
question depends largely on one's estimate of the future of
the secularized forms of Western culture. Are they as
securely rooted in themselves, in the axioms of natural law,
and in the principle of the autonomy of reason as it was
supposed in the beginnings of modernity? Not only the
seventeenth-century pioneers of a reconstruction of the
social world on the basis of the concept of human nature
saw this to be so; those who followed took for granted the
solidity of those foundations with even more confidence in
the course of the following centuries. Until very recently it
was considered inevitable that the progressive dynamic of
Western scientific and technological civilization would
spread throughout the entire world, since unlimited extrapolation of the European process of secularization seemed
plausible. In such a perspective the absence of God in
modern secular culture had to be taken as definitive, and the
imaginative phrase "death of God" commended itself as a
short formula for this state of affairs. As long as such an
extrapolation of cultural development is accepted, the mar-
ginalization of all religion must appear inevitable. Adaptation to the standards of secular culture, the transformation
of the residual energies of religious consciousness into

ethical and social motivation, may appear to be the only alternative to an unproductive withdrawal that would preserve traditional forms of worship and belief through petrifaction. This estimate of the secular culture as bearing the future of humankind has had a vast impact to the present day and has produced deep insecurity among the faithful, especially among those to whom the continuation of the Christian tradition is entrusted. The very fact that the "death of God" could become a serious issue in theology is understandable only from the perspective of this cultural development. Certainly, the kenotic interpretation of the notion of the death of God in terms of an action of God himself, sacrificing himself for the sake of human redemption and freedom, represents an amazing attempt to interpret even the atheism of modern secular culture as determined by that God whose jurisdiction this culture wanted to cast off. Presenting the very process of emancipation from God as an action *of* that God is equivalent in cultural philosophy to the function of deism in earlier centuries over against the mechanistic world view of modern physics which left no room for divine interference in the course of natural processes and only allowed for the conception of a divine engineer who put himself out of work by the very perfection of his self-regulative creation. A theology with a definitive "death" of God as well as a perhaps only temporary absence from his rule explains the phenomenon of God's absence in modern culture by attributing the very loss of divine function to an action of that God. This is what distinguishes these interpretations from atheistic thought in the proper sense of the word. Even if interested in religious life and especially in Christianity, atheistic thinkers—like Bloch—never consider it as evidence of a divine activity, but at most as some progress toward human self-realization, the true nature of which is still concealed from the religious person. It is for this reason that, remarkably enough, Bloch made no use of Hegel's idea of the incarnation as death of God. Nevertheless, the so-called theology of the death of God was a phenomenon of adaptation in that it presupposed as a matter of fact the unlimited and continuing development of modern secular culture. Rather than receiving that secular optimism with skeptical reserve, the theologians of the death of God reformulated traditional theology in such a way as to make it compatible—even at the price of a heavy loss of theological substance—with that supposedly inevitable direction of cultural development. Some of them thought in this way to preserve the particularity of the Christian faith over against merely human religion and to complete the tendency of modern theology toward Christological concentration. But the attacks on the concept of religion that became customary in dialectical theology and among its heirs is itself a result of a problematic adaptation to the spirit of the age. Thus the atheist critique of religion and the concentration on Jesus Christ that led to the replacement of God by the human person of Jesus turned out to be inadequate in view of the fact that, as Vahanian had already noticed, Jesus always supposed the existence of the God of Israel, whom he called his Father and from whom he derived his mission. On balance, then, the theology of the death of God must inevitably be considered an example of excessive adaptation to the spirit of a culture without God, and its rise is only understandable on the premise that this secular culture will persist and continue to grow by its own intrinsic power.

It is precisely this premise which appears doubtful today. There is, in the first place, the judgment of modern sociology of religion that the principle of a complete neutrality of the state in questions of religion is somewhat illusory, because any political order of society needs legitimation and must rest its legitimation upon some truth that is at least believed to be beyond manipulation. In modern times the legitimating agencies, because of the prejudice that religion can be a matter of private confession only, have been conceived of predominantly in the quasi-scientific language of modern ideologies. Nevertheless, their function has been that of religious legitimation, and deceptions in that issue can entail grave consequences for the state and its relation to explicitly religious institutions, as well as for those institutions themselves. The most incisive consequence of the presumed religious neutrality of the state and of the public culture may be that all agencies that provide meaning to human life become a matter of purely subjective discretion, from religion through art and higher education and all the way to morals. People become accustomed to relate to all of them by way of a consumer's attitude that destroys the awareness of meaning. Therefore secular culture, the more it develops without restriction, produces the experience of meaninglessness first in public life and finally also in individual life. The dissolution of the traditional institutions of social life including family and marriage for the sake of promoting the emancipation of the individual leaves that individual to the fate of increasing loneliness in the midst of a noisy machinery of "communication," an experience described time and again by modern literature since Samuel Beckett (b. 1906) and Gottfried Benn (1886–1956). That loneliness is most obvious and most paradoxical in the transformation of erotic relations into changing, temporary, and exchangeable partnerships. As a consequence of that increasing experience of loneliness, fewer persons are able to develop a sense of personal identity in the course of their individual lives, and that entails the spread of neurosis. At the end of such a journey into loneliness there emerge the recourse to violence and terror on the one hand, and the resort to suicide on the other.

It is not likely that secular societies will be able in the long run to survive the consequences of the much-touted emancipation of the individual. In some parts of the world, secular culture survives because it lives off the substance of whatever in Christian tradition and morals has not yet been used up in the process of secularization. In other regions, quasi-religious roots of national traditional identity, in addition to the traditional religions or to new ideologies, withstand the forces of secularization. It is good to consider, however, that the different replacements for religious meaning are usually more susceptible to disintegration by reduction to the arbitrariness of human values than is religion itself. There is therefore less reason for concern over the future of religion than many until recently assumed. This also applies to Christianity, which is not so closely tied to Western secular culture that the crisis of that culture would threaten its future.

Considerations like these lead to a significant change in the framework for evaluating the phenomenon of the absence of God in modern secular culture. Since the future of cultural development is no longer so securely owned by secularization as was supposed a century ago, or even some decades ago, the phenomenon of the absence of God in modern secular culture appears more as a problem of that culture than as an indication of a possible end to the history of Christianity. Our cultural world, it seems is in acute danger of dying because of the absence of God, if human persons continue to seek in vain for meaning in their personal lives, if increasing numbers fail to develop a sense of their personal identity, if the flood of neurosis continues to rise, if more and more people take refuge in suicide or violence, and if the state continues to lose its legitimacy in the consciousness of the citizens, while the cultural tradition functions according to the rules of supply at the discretion of individual demand. All these are the consequences of the absence of God. But far from indicating the death of God, they suggest, rather, that God is not neglected with impunity.

In the Bible the absence of God usually indicates that his judgment is at hand. This judgment of God does not consist, of course, of arbitrary punishments, but means that God leaves sinners to the consequences of their own deeds, as the apostle Paul says (Rom. 1:24ff.). Since the sustaining presence of God is necessary for all creatures to survive, his absense means danger. Therefore the psalm says of the creatures, "When thou hidest thy face, they are dismayed" (Ps. 104:29), and therefore the religious Jew prays, "Hide not thy face from me, lest I be like those who go down to the Pit" (Ps. 143:7; see also Ps. 10:1ff.; 22:24; 44:24; 69:17). When God hides his face and leaves his human creatures to their own devices, it is not an indication of weakness but an expression of his wrath (Ps. 89:46; cf. Job 13:24). Thus the prophet Isaiah received the rejection of his message as an effect of God's hiding from his people and therefore as an omen of impending judgment prepared for by their obdurateness. Ezekiel saw in a vision that God departed from the Jerusalem Temple, leaving the Temple and the city to speedy destruction by the Babylonians. Later on at Golgotha the absence of God and the godforsakenness of Jesus comprised the darkness of the divine judgment that Jesus bore in our place. If all this is taken into consideration, it must appear frivolous to interpret the absence of God in modern secular culture, as even theologians did, as suggesting that God might perhaps be dead. On the contrary, the experience of the absence of God should alert every serious observer to sound an alarm, not so much for God, or for the future of Christianity, but for Western secular culture with its proud science and technology. At present the symptoms of its decay are unmistakable, but it is too easily overlooked that this decay is the consequence of the absence of God, and that this absence effectuates the divine judgment that is the consequence of human neglect.

The darkness of the absence of God is most dense where it is not even perceived. Contemporary literature and art describe its consequences: the loss of a personal expression in the faces of people and the decomposition of human lives deprived of personal identity; the breakup of human communication and of erotic relations, resulting in loneliness and eruptions of that loneliness in assaults of excessive pity for oneself, in terror against others, and finally in suicide. Even the absence of God as such becomes an issue here and there, the feeling of an "empty transcendence," as H. Friedrich described it, especially in modern French poetry, but also in the German poet Gottfried Benn. Even the treatment of religious topics in modern literature turns to the phenomenon of the absence of God, as in Georges Bernanos or Graham Greene. But wherever persons discover the absence of God in the midst of their sufferings, and at the same time (this seems to happen more rarely) wherever they recognize God's absence as evidence of divine judgment and as a consequence of their own behavior, there God is no longer completely absent. There his presence makes itself felt again. And God's presence to the one who seeks his presence means recovery.

V
A Search
for the
Authentic Self

THE PROCESS of continuing modernization in the secularized societies of the Western world has produced increasingly widespread and intense feelings of alienation among their individual members. The development of industrialization and bureaucratization presents modern society to the individual as an immensely complicated and anonymous system that does not care for the personal needs and problems of the individual. As traditional social structures such as the family, where the individual occupied a meaningful place, dissolve or lose their power as centers of orientation, the individual often feels homeless and abandoned in the personal center of his or her life.[50] Personal identity becomes a problem. Many seek to solve such problems with the aid of the psychologist, but others become aware that the meaningful life they yearn for is not something they can create for themselves. Every part of the content of life that the ego may decide upon can seem trite merely because it depends on arbitrary choice. When the ego itself thus comes under suspicion, a person may find peace in the message of Buddhism and through the practice of Buddhist meditation on the transitoriness of the ego, of its arbitrary concerns, and of its suffering in an unyielding world. The promise of such peace, of course, is offered more generally to anyone concerned for personal identity, for the authentic self. Thus Buddhist teaching and psychoanalysis seem to have a common border. But their territories are different. While the psychotherapist wants to strengthen the ego, Buddhism calls us to resign its claims and concerns. This, we are told, is the only way to discover our true, authentic self and attain permanent peace.[51]

Buddhist spirituality seems remarkably relevant to the spiritual needs of the alienated human individual in modern secular society. It seems to offer a more suitable answer to those needs than the penitential piety that pervades many forms of traditional Christianity. Buddhist teaching does not first of all urge the individual to confess to being a sinner, responsible for the miserable condition of his or her own life and its social context. Although the call to penitence puts considerable strain on the individual, it often fails to correspond to genuine experience, which in the modern world in general suggests rather the powerlessness of the individual over against an anonymous system. In private life moral standards have been weakened or dissolved as a consequence of the pluralization of individual life-styles. To many individuals, therefore, their own sinfulness is not an obvious experience, though they may still persuade themselves that it is so. On the other hand, there are problems of personal identity that need not be artificially produced, but occur with obtrusive evidence. Christianity should address its message more consciously to this level of experience. The concept of sin does not belong, in the first place, to the immediacy of personal experience, but rather to the *explanation* of such experience. It is not to be denied that someone may genuinely experience being a sinner, but that constitutes a special case. If such experience means more than occasional violations of specific provisions of divine law that first of all have to be accepted as such, then the experience of oneself as a sinner presupposes the interiorization of a particular description of human subjectivity. In the medieval church and at the time of the Reformation some degree of such interiorization of the Christian doctrine of sin could be generally presupposed. This being no longer the case, it is not very effective to call upon the individual experience of sin to provide an experiential basis on which to argue for other Christian assertions. Recognizing this situation does not deprive the doctrine of sin of its descriptive and explanatory value. Its descriptive use, however, applies to the structure of human subjectivity, which it presupposes, and here it is that we get to the experiential level, since human subjectivity is distinguished by its including some form of self-awareness.

The anthropological analysis of the human self provides an appropriate meeting ground for the dialogue between Christianity and Buddhism. This may apply in some degree to the dialogue with other religions as well, but the case of Buddhism is a special one. A discussion with Judaism and Islam would need to focus much more directly on the idea of God, while in the dialogue with Hinduism anthropological questions are subordinate to the discussion of the character of reality in general. These questions may also stand in the background of the dialogue between Christianity and Buddhism. These two religions conceive the relation of the human person to the world of nature in profoundly different ways.[52] We shall focus here on anthropology in particular rather than on cosmology, because both religions, though in different ways, promise liberation of the human person from bondage in this world.

Roughly twenty years ago, Paul Tillich described the difference between Christianity and Buddhism as a difference in answering "the question of the intrinsic aim of existence." While in Christianity the *telos,* or *goal,* is the kingdom of God, in Buddhism it is, according to Tillich, Nirvana.[53] This formula, although objectionable, contained an important element of truth, to which we shall return later. There may be also an element of truth in contrasting Christianity and Buddhism, as Tillich did in this connection, as a personalistic versus a transpersonal "ontological" way of thought. But this may also be misleading. Christian language about the human condition is not merely ethical. Tillich, in this respect, was too heavily influenced by Ernst Troeltsch's way of contrasting the "ethical" religions of the West to the "ontological" religions of the East. It is not primarily "the *aim* of existence" on which the two religions differ, but the *structure* of existence, especially of human existence, of human subjectivity. In fact, Tillich himself, in his structural analysis of subjectivity, provided categories that could be used by a modern Buddhist to present the Buddhist position and criticize the Christian one.

Shin'ichi Hisamatsu in an article on atheism discusses Christianity by distinguishing three types of religion: medieval "heteronomous" religion, modern "autonomy," and postmodern "heteronomous" autonomy.[54] While heteronomous religion was characterized by an uncritical acceptance of authority, the modern autonomous self is critical of traditional authorities though still uncritical in relation to itself. It does not ask the question of the nature and constitution of the human ego. Now the structure of the ego includes an element of negativity, of self-abnegation, in knowing itself as a finite subject that cannot constitute itself. The awareness of this negativity points beyond the ego to a quasi-"heteronomous" constitution of the ego by, say, some absolute subject. Hisamatsu then establishes a connection between this quasi-"heteronomous" constitution of the ego and the Buddhist teaching that the true self, the enlightened self, is different and yet at the same time not different from the empirical self or ego.

Hisamatsu's typological scheme can hardly fail to strike a Christian by its similarity to Paul Tillich's typology of

heteronomous, autonomous, and theonomous culture.[55] It
has been shown recently that the entire development of
Tillich's thought was motivated by his concern for a religious reconstitution of human subjectivity that would transcend the autonomous subject and regenerate it and its
cultural world on the basis of the divine ground of being.[56]
Tillich's later preference for an ontological language thus
appears as just another phase in his struggle for a theonomous culture. However, although he started from studies in
German idealism, Tillich did not concentrate his efforts on
the structure of subjectivity as such. Perhaps the reason for
this is that Tillich envisioned the realization of human
destiny in the communal life of culture rather than in the
solitary individual. In the end, in his *Systematic Theology,*
he did offer a model describing the structure of subjectivity
in terms of his ontological language, but then his talk of
essence and existence remained half mythological. The lack
of a consistent theory integrating autonomous subjectivity
into a theonomous interpretation of the human person may
explain the otherwise puzzling fact that Tillich did not bring
his concept of theonomy versus autonomy to bear on his
comparison between Christianity and Buddhism, but remained dependent on the scheme of contrasting ethical to
ontological religion. His concept of theonomy versus autonomy could have opened the path to a more profound
analysis of the Buddhist philosophy of the self and to a more
incisive critique of the modern principle of autonomous
subjectivity.

In comparing the two religions, the Buddhist philosopher
Masao Abe said in a recent essay that Buddhist awakening
and Christian conversion agree "in so far as the death of the
human ego is essential to salvation."[57] In view of the
Pauline ideas he had in mind, this statement is understandable. The apostle asserted quite unambiguously that the
only way to salvation is to die with Christ in the hope of

being raised together with him. But the anthropological implications of this view were rarely spelled out in Christian thought. Does Paul not imply that only the new Adam reveals the true self of the human person, that is to say, the destiny of humanity as created in the image of God? What is to be said, then, about the empirical self or ego? Who is the "inmost self" of Rom. 7:22, the self that is said to take delight in the law of God? Is it what we call the empirical subject? Or is it the new Adam? The second assumption would suggest that in Romans 7 Paul talks about the struggle within the reborn Christian person, as Luther assumed. But even if we accept the contrasting conclusion of modern exegesis that Paul is talking in this chapter about the conflict within the human person prior to conversion to Christ, still that "inmost self" is not to be equated with the ego of the so-called "natural man." Rather, it is the human person as seen in the light of that person's destiny to salvation in Christ. Seen in that perspective, the ego of the person I have been is profoundly different from what I now consider myself to be, and yet it is identical. In identifying with an alienated personal past, the Christian supposes a hidden presence of the true self, even in the struggle of the old Adam, and retrospectively calls on the evidence of traces there of the presence of the true self now enjoyed—for these traces bear witness to the Christian identity that liberates the "inmost self" of the former person.

The radical implications of this Pauline view were but faintly appropriated by later Christian anthropology. The temporal perspective on the identity of the self was especially neglected. While in Paul the Christian identifies himself in the story of the old Adam differently than the old Adam might have done, later Christian thought located the "inmost self" of Romans 7 in the faculty of reason as if that "inmost self" would always remain the same. Still, it was admitted that the natural person is transcended by grace.

But the gift of grace was interpreted as some additional supernatural quality granted to the personal self already in existence rather than as a reconstitution of that personal center itself. Especially in Western Christian thought the human person as rational individual and subject of free choice was considered the continuous basis for the process of salvation, and it was this that became the target of Luther's criticism. Even in relation to grace, the free will of the natural person had been given a position of importance that Luther thought incompatible with the New Testament, especially with Pauline theology. Luther rediscovered that in the event of regeneration according to Paul not only some quality of the subject but the subject itself is changed. That is the significance of Luther's famous phrase when he says that we are justified "outside ourselves" in Christ, *extra nos in Christo*. He means outside our old "self."[58] It is the power of faith that it places us outside ourselves, because in the act of trust our existence is built on the one to whom we entrust ourselves, to whom we quite literally leave ourselves. However, because such is the power of faith, the act of faith cannot adequately be understood as an action of the old subject, since that is to be left behind in the act. Luther therefore liked to describe faith as an event of *rapture,* of spiritual ecstasy carrying us beyond ourselves.[59] It is from this point of view that we must understand Luther's struggle against free will. Luther did not deny that choice is always a distinctive mark of the human person, but he restricted its range to the limitations of the acting subject itself. It is not within the scope of that subject to become a radically new person. But precisely this happens through faith in Christ. In him we find our true freedom, the authentic self beyond what we were before. And yet, because of the saving love and promise of Christ offered to the sinner, it is our own self, the true identity of the person we were even before, now finally achieved, liberated not from some external bondage but from bondage to our old self.

In the history of Christian thought, Luther's anthropology is distinguished by rediscovering and interpreting the anthropological radicalism implicit in Pauline theology. One may wonder why this had not been realized before Luther, and one answer to this question is that the opposite view had also been developed on the basis of a particularly Christian, if different, concern. This was the concern for the individual human person and for its eternal value, a concern that reaches back to the teaching of Jesus himself. It was expressed in the parables of the lost sheep and the prodigal son. It prompted Christian thinkers to conceive of each individual as an immortal subject. (The very notion of the subject, in the modern sense of the word, emerged that way.) And in analogy to God's creative freedom, the subjectivity of the human person created in the image of God was thought to culminate in the act of free decision. But the more these ideas were conceived in terms of timeless structure, the less it remained possible to do full justice to the radical transformation that occurs in the act of faith and is symbolized in the rite of baptism.

In the course of modern history and modern thought, traditional Christian personalism, reempowered by developments in the doctrines of natural law and political philosophy, prevailed over Luther's profound new anthropological insights. On the contemporary scene, however, the traditional view of individual freedom, though still dominant, seems increasingly beset by difficulties because of the growing awareness of the social conditions of human identity and, even more important, because of the potentially epidemic feeling of the shallow, arbitrary character of formal freedom, which deprives our Western discourse about freedom of its self-confidence.

One of the shortcomings of traditional Christian personalism in the present situation is that it seems impracticable on such a basis to arrive at a meaningful dialogue with Buddhism. Among other things, it is the weakness of traditional Christian personalism that accounts for the attractiveness of Buddhist ideas to contemporary Western culture. In many ways, the Buddhist teaching about the human self seems more profound and more realistic than the dominant Western ideology of individual freedom. In this situation, a genuinely Lutheran anthropology offers a more effective vehicle for meeting the challenge of Buddhism, because Buddhism and the Lutheran version of Christian anthropology have a common meeting ground in the awareness, described by Masao Abe, that "the death of the human ego is essential to salvation," or, in more general terms, that the natural ego is not yet the true self of the human person. Buddhist criticism of the superficial character of current Western ideals of human freedom should remind Lutherans of Luther's criticism of the doctrine of free will and should encourage them to reappropriate Luther's critical stance toward the humanistic origins of the modern philosophy of freedom.

Convergence between Lutheran and Buddhist perspectives in their critical evaluation of the natural ego's self-affirmation does not mean, of course, that there would remain no important difference between the two religions. According to Masao Abe, the basic difference between Christianity and Buddhism is that the Christian faith relates to Jesus Christ as a transcendent reality, while Buddhism denies any form of dualism, especially that of subject and object. The Buddhist, therefore, does not deny the ego in favor of a transcendent Thou, but must "kill" the authority of the Buddha as well, and must even deny the opposition of Nirvana to Samsara, because of the necessity to transcend every form of dualism and opposition.[60]

In such a radical way, to be sure, this may be true only of

Zen, while Jodo-Shin in its emphasis on Amida offers a different picture. One remembers that even Karl Barth was struck by the similarity between this form of Buddhism and Protestant belief in justification by faith alone.[61] However, Katsumi Takizawa, the leading Japanese Christian theologian, recently cautioned against overestimating the difference between the two Buddhist schools on this point.[62] Takizawa argues that the figure of Amida in Shinran's view is not really something totally other over against the ego of the believer, while on the other hand the meditational techniques of Zen were considered by Dogen not so much the work of the individual self but rather that of the one true Dharma active in the individual. In this interpretation, both schools are loyal to Buddhist principles by negating both sides of the dualism of subject and object. But what about Christianity? Does not the Christian faith, especially in its Lutheran form, emphatically assert the reality of the other, of Jesus Christ and of God, while transcending the ego of the believer? Are we not here touching the basic structural difference between the two religions, the most solemn expression of which is that the Christian believes in a transcendent God while the Buddhist's ultimate wisdom is emptiness, Sunyata?

At this point, it seems particularly important to avoid a premature assessment. Masao Abe, in an earlier essay, admitted that there is no undifferentiated objectivism concerning the divine reality, even in Christianity. He especially noticed that in Jesus' proclamation "the Kingdom of God is not simply transcendent" but "is both immanent and transcendent," because it is still in the future while also present already.[63] The Christian theologian can only confirm this observation of the Buddhist author, an observation that receives additional weight in view of the fact that God himself cannot be separated from his kingdom. This element of truth was already present in Bultmann's contention that objectifying language in relation to God is misleading. On the other hand, if subjectivism is to be avoided, one must begin with objectifying language about God, keeping in mind all the while that the particular subject matter will compel us to transcend mere objectivism.

Masao Abe has also noticed that a similar structure as in the message of the kingdom can be discerned in Christology. The dogma of the incarnation expresses the negation of the mere otherness of God so that Christ becomes a symbol of "transcending even the religious transcendence." This, according to Abe, is comparable to the negation of Nirvana as opposed to Samsara in Mahayana Buddhism. And turning from the dogma to the person of Christ, Abe refers to the famous phrase of Paul in Phil. 2:7 that Christ Jesus "emptied himself, taking the form of a servant." He interprets this phrase by attributing "kenotic" self-abnegation to the historical person of Jesus Christ as the Lutheran theologians of the seventeenth century did. In doing so, he contradicts the contention of modern exegesis that in Philippians 2 the self-emptying activity is that of the divine Logos in the event of the incarnation, which then constitutes the historical person of Jesus Christ. According to Abe, the passage shows that "Jesus Christ is God who became flesh by emptying or abnegating Himself even unto death." And since it is through this *kenotic* negation that "the immanent and the transcendent became identical in Jesus Christ," the Buddhist can even call him "the Christian symbol of Ultimate Reality." And yet, in Abe's judgment the Christian affirmation that this "paradoxical oneness was realized in history only in Jesus Christ" separates Christianity and Buddhism. Abe therefore concludes that a kind of objectification still remains, because "the relation between Christ and the believer is dualistic."[64]

At this point we turn again to Luther, whose thought on Christ's self-abnegation shows that the judgment of the perceptive and sympathetic Buddhist critic of Christianity needs further qualification. According to Luther, Christ, in taking upon himself the judgment of God, prefigured the path of self-abnegation which the Christian must follow in order to enjoy communion with Christ. Thus, *like* Christ, the believer will have communion with God through justifying God in his judgments. But this self-abnegation of the Christian happens, according to Luther, in the act of faith. Hence, the relation between Christ and the believer is not dualistic, as Abe assumes. On the contrary, it is characterized by *conformity* with Christ on the part of the believer, as it is characterized on the part of Jesus Christ by the service of self-giving love. And since the individual believer cannot continue in such conformity with Christ without also participating in the love of Christ in relation to others, the unity between Christ and the believer also includes the community of the faithful, the church. This unity is expressed in the description of the church as the body of Christ. It is, to be sure, not a unity without differentiation. As Jesus discriminated himself from the Father in accepting the Father's commission and judgment, so the believer discriminates his or her own person from Jesus in accepting his service and promise. But precisely because of such self-differentiation there is communion between the Son and the Father, and also between the believer and Jesus Christ.

Certainly these considerations go beyond Luther's own explicit statements, not simply repeating them, and not commenting on them in terms of historical interpretation, but attempting to explicate their implicit structure in a generalized way. In his Christological statements, especially in his early writings and lecture courses, Luther differed from the bulk of medieval theology by intimately relating the humility of Christ to the humility of the faithful, and from this sort of description there emerged the intuition of a spiritual unity of the believer with Christ that remained fundamental to Luther's doctrine of justification. Thus, Luther's theology does not exhibit a dualistic conception of the relationship between Jesus Christ and the community of Christians. There is an element of differentiation, of course, but it is integrated into an encompassing unity. The ultimate locus for treating this interpenetration of differentiation and unity has always been, in the history of Christian thought, the doctrine of the Trinity. Luther did not attempt a systematic reconstruction of Trinitarian doctrine, but he was obviously inclined not to separate the Trinity from the history of salvation, but to keep these two issues together. In such a perspective, however, the anthropological and the Christological aspects of differentiation and unity are integrated into their most comprehensive frame of reference, and on this level of Trinitarian doctrine, then, the dispute between Christianity and Buddhism concerning whether Christianity is guilty of some form of dualism must be settled. Christianity can withstand the Buddhist critique of dualism only if the Trinity is not set apart from creation and salvation history but is explained as the Christian answer to the question of how God and the world can be different in such a way that each is nevertheless not separate from the other. The dialogue that begins on the level of anthropology, with the search for the authentic self of the human person, can approach completion only in a discussion of the nature of ultimate reality, as soon as the need to transcend the difference between subject and object, the ego and the world, is introduced with the question of how to obtain self-identity.

Even so, the differences between the two religions demand further clarification. Even a Buddhist partner who is convinced that the Christian view should not be characterized as dualistic will continue to wonder why Christianity so vehemently insists on the uniqueness of a historical person. Masao Abe touches upon this difference in saying that "identification with Christ as Ultimate Reality" in the act of faith is "the quintessence of Christian faith. The essence of Zen, however, is not identification with Christ or with Buddha, but identification with emptiness."[65]

At this point, the Christian might be tempted to turn Buddhist criticism on its master by asking whether perhaps even emptiness itself is a dualistic notion. Now this question can take both a naive and a more sophisticated form. The naive inquiry begins with the apparent difference between the enlightened and the unenlightened life, but confuses it with the conceptual difference between Nirvana and Samsara. The question put in this form, then, goes like this: Is not the wisdom of the wise and the Nirvana of the wise still opposed to the world of emergence and decay, the world of Samsara? The inconsiderate questioner will quickly be reminded that even the opposition of Nirvana to Samsara is a dualism to be negated, in which case Nirvana coincides with Samsara and "emptiness" means precisely this coincidence, not an alternative reality to the everyday world of Samsara. The question may then reappear in a second, more sophisticated form relating to the movement of negation as such: Does not the movement of negation inevitably constitute a new opposition at each turn?[66] At first the world of genesis and decay is negated together with the empirical ego, and Nirvana results as opposed to the duality of ego and Samsara. Then Nirvana itself is negated as opposed to Samsara, and emptiness results. But is not the notion of emptiness, then, again opposed to the duality of Nirvana and Samsara, thereby creating a new form of dualism, the dualism between enlightened and unenlightened life in the world of Samsara? Even if that dualism could be overcome on the next level, the form of negation as such seems to produce a new opposition at each turn.

Such iteration of dualistic opposition seems unavoidable except in that the positive meaning of negating the negative is not considered a product of human reflection, but rather an event of rapture that carries us beyond ourselves, just as Luther envisioned the spiritual event of faith. But then, does not such an occurrence display some sort of activity, an activity that overwhelms us? If that is the case, however, some idea of divine reality that seizes us in such an experience seems already involved. The history of Buddhism itself in its Mahayana period suggests that the intuition of divine reality reenters the scene as soon as the transition is made from the method of incessant negation to the positive reality that becomes present in negating the negative.

In Christianity the mystery of divine involvement in the positive actuality of life is seen as "affirmative" of human existence. That means that God "affirms" concrete individual existence and that he does so in some way eternally. That is what Luther called the Word of Promise, which epitomizes God's relation to his creation. Only a few of the numerous corollaries to that overwhelmingly affirmative experience can be mentioned: In the *first* place, it implies that the absolute reality is not only considered in some sense active, and therefore personal, but also reliable, just as the image of a loving father suggests. *Second,* the awareness of the divine as overwhelmingly affirmative of finite existence implies not only that the presence of God in Jesus Christ is definitive, but that in similar ways the historically unique in every individual life is important to the degree that the divine affirmation of finite reality encourages hope for a definitive future of individual existence beyond this transitory state, the hope for a resurrection of the dead and for a renewed heaven and earth. Thus it seems to be the Christian sense for the affirmative character of the divine that explains some of the peculiarities of the Christian faith that are most puzzling to the Buddhist, particularly the emphasis on the unique importance of the historical person of Jesus Christ. This is to be understood in the context of the affirmative evaluation of the historical in general, with due attention to each particular case.

The difference between the Christian affirmation of the reality of life and the attitude of the Mahayana tradition seems to become apparent especially in the Christian eschatological hope. The Christian affirmation not only accepts the reality of Samsara as it is in its transitoriness but aims at a final victory over both death and transitoriness. The Christian affirmation is marked by a transformative thrust, and the dynamics of transformation come to the fore in Christian ethics as well as in eschatological hope. Even the special place assigned to the human person in the world of nature and to the human species as champion of the future salvation of all creation (Rom. 8:19ff.) must be understood in connection with Christian longing for the transfiguration of this world into the glory of God.

It is precisely the transformative impulse in Christianity which also produced, as in the Jewish tradition earlier, an emphasis on sin and sinfulness. Sin is the common denominator of everything that resists the spirit of transformation into the glory of God. Sin resists this spirit inside the human person who is called in such a peculiar way to act as its agent in the world. Along with the perishableness of death, therefore, suffering and disease and—even before them— sin must be overcome. This explains the important place sin occupies in traditional Christian piety. It also explains how the affirmative nature of the Christian spirit can virtually disappear in morose worry over one's sinful condition as also perversely in justifying oneself by confessing oneself a sinner.

We need not deal here with the different forms which that perversion of the Christian spirit can take. It may be sufficient to state that the doctrine of sin appears in its genuine form as a companion of the affirmative message of

Christianity, because that affirmation is transformative and imparts a perspective of temporal and historical process. This is also the reason why the liberation and identity that the gospel of God's affirmation of his creature conveys to the human person is appropriated only by faith. But by faith that affirmation and its joy become present in the human person even now. The distinctive importance of the notion of faith in Christianity is due to the transformative and therefore historical character of the divine affirmation of the individual. For this reason the identity of the human person, the authentic self, is realized outside ourselves in Christ, as Luther said, and this perspective allows Christian teaching to include also the human experience of nonidentity and inauthenticity in its interpretation of the human predicament. Thus it can do justice to the history of the individual in search of the true self, which nevertheless is already present in some way in this same process.

What contribution does the Lutheran tradition offer to the Christian dialogue with Buddhism? The basic contribution should be recognized in its convergence with the Buddhist critique of the self-affirmation of the empirical ego. Beyond that the Lutheran tradition has to offer a positive vision of how authentic self-identity is constituted by faith in Christ. It seems possible to answer Buddhist criticism of traditional Christian doctrine by pointing out that the Christian emphasis on Christ belongs to the spectrum of transformative affirmation as epitomizing the Christian conception of the impingement of ultimate reality upon the human person. The Lutheran doctrine of justification by faith teaches nothing else but the transformative affirmation of the human person by God's love. Such a way of explaining Christian doctrine establishes contact with the Buddhist teaching of the Mahayana tradition, which turned from the negation of the world of Samsara—including the human self—to the negation of the opposition of Nirvana to Samsara, resulting in the doctrine of emptiness as a liberated existence in the midst of the transitory world of Samsara. The Lutheran doctrine of justification by faith in Christ can help to articulate the Christian form of such affirmation of finite existence in distinction from Buddhism. The challenge of Buddhism in focusing on the experience of the human self, on the other hand, may help the Christian (and especially the Lutheran Christian) to overcome the overemphasis on sin and penitential piety that has tended to pervert the Christian *euangelion* and to deprive it of its joy and radiant enthusiasm. It is not true—as the pietistic tradition assumed—that on the basis of immediate awareness every individual, if honest, should admit his or her sinfulness. Rather, it is only retrospectively, on the basis of a Christian understanding of ourselves, that we identify a certain structure of behavior as sinful.

Notes

1. Friedrich Nietzsche, *Genealogy of Morals*, II.
2. Ibid., II, xx.
3. Nietzsche, *Genealogy of Morals*, III.
4. Sigmund Freud, *Totem and Taboo*, III, 4.
5. Nietzsche, *Genealogy of Morals*, II, ix.
6. Freud, *Totem and Taboo*, III, 4.
7. See the explanation of this phrase by W. Joest, *Ontologie der Person bei Luther* (Göttingen: Vandenhoeck & Ruprecht, 1967), pp. 233–274.
8. See, e.g., Augustine, *De civ. Dei* X.5: . . . sacramentum, id est sacrum signum; cf. Thomas Aquinas, *Summa Theol.* III.60.1; John Calvin, *Institutes of the Christian Religion* (1559), IV.14.18.
9. *Weimarer Ausgabe, D. Martin Luthers Werke* (hereafter *WA*) 2, 742–758, esp. 743 and 754.
10. *WA* 2, 748.
11. *WA* 5, 353–378, esp. 356f., 359, 374, 376; cf. *WA* 2, 744. It was as a consequence of this emphasis that Luther now could declare that in the Eucharist the words are far more important than the material symbols of bread and wine (*WA* 6, 363; cf. 374).
12. Karl Barth, *Der Römerbrief*, 2d ed. (1922), pp. 459ff. (E.T. *The Epistle to the Romans*, tr. by Edwyn C. Hoskyns; London: Oxford University Press, 1933.)
13. Karl Barth, *Christengemeinde und Bürgergemeinde*, Theologische Studien 20 (Bielefeld, 1946), pp. 32f. (n. 17). (E.T. in Karl Barth, *Against the Stream;* London: SCM Press, 1954.)
14. Jürgen Moltmann, *Theologie der Hoffnung* (Munich: Chr. Kaiser Verlag, 1964), pp. 272, 303.
15. Jürgen Moltmann, *Der gekreuzigte Gott* (1972), p. 309. (E.T. *The Crucified God;* Harper & Row, 1974.) Cf. also his article "Die

Revolution der Freiheit," in *Perspektiven der Theologie* (1968), pp. 189–211, esp. 202ff.

16. Gustavo Gutiérrez, *Theologie der Befreiung* (1972), pp. 190ff. (E.T. *A Theology of Liberation;* Orbis Books, 1971.) For the relation of this new spirituality of liberation to Latin American popular piety, see the article of José Miguez-Bonino on this subject in *Concilium* 10 (1974), pp. 455ff.

17. See, e.g., Norman Cohn, *The Pursuit of the Millennium: Revolutionary Millenarians and Mystical Anarchists of the Middle Ages* (1957); rev. and enl. ed. (Oxford University Press, 1970), esp. pp. 53ff., 198ff., 223ff.

18. Ernst Troeltsch, *Die Soziallehren der christlichen Kirchen und Gruppen* (1912), pp. 733ff. (E.T. *The Social Teachings of the Christian Churches;* Macmillan Co., 1931.)

19. More on this subject in the article on Luther's doctrine of the two kingdoms in my *Ethics* (Westminster Press, 1981), pp. 112–131.

20. This problem has been investigated with special care by Wilfred Joest, *Gesetz und Freiheit. Das Problem des tertius usus legis bei Luther und die neutestamentliche Parainese* (1951; 2d ed., 1956), pp. 65ff., 68ff.

21. See Werner Krusche, *Das Wirken des Heiligen Geistes nach Calvin* (1957), pp. 275ff., also 265ff.

22. Ibid., pp. 245ff. and esp. 253f. (Calvin's commentary on II Thess. 2:13). See also Calvin, *Inst.* III.14.18f.

23. Calvin, *Inst.* IV.11.5 and IV.12.2.

24. See Krusche, *Das Wirken des Heiligen Geistes nach Calvin,* pp. 110ff.

25. Ibid., pp. 333ff.

26. Wilhelm Niesel, *Die Theologie Calvins* (1938; 2d ed., 1957), p. 228, esp. on *Corpus Reformatorum* 13, 69.17, and 14, 342. (E.T. *The Theology of Calvin;* Westminster Press, 1956.) See also *Inst.* IV.20.5.

27. Niesel, *Die Theologie Calvins,* pp. 229ff. See also *Inst.* IV.20.9.

28. *Corpus Reformatorum* 43, 374. See also *Inst.* IV.20.8: Atque, ut libenter fateor nullum esse gubernationis genus isto beatius, ubi libertas ad eam quam decet moderationem est composita . . . Quin etiam huc summa diligentia intenti magistratus esse debent, ne qua in parte libertatem, cuius praesides sunt constituti, minui, nedum violari patiantur. ("And, as I freely admit that no kind of government is more happy than one where freedom is regulated with becoming moderation . . . Indeed, the magistrates

ought to apply themselves with the highest diligence to prevent the freedom (whose guardians they have been appointed) from being in any respect diminished, far less be violated." *Calvin: Institutes of the Christian Religion,* ed. by John T. McNeill, tr. by Ford Lewis Battles; Vol. 2, p. 1494; Westminster Press, 1960.)

29. See Krusche, *Das Wirken des Heiligen Geistes nach Calvin,* pp. 114ff., and the literature discussed there.

30. James L. Adams, "Theokratie, Kapitalismus und Demokratie," *Zeitschrift für Evangelische Ethik* 12 (1968), pp. 247–267, esp. 252f. Michael Walzer, *The Revolution of the Saints: A Study in the Origins of Radical Politics* (Harvard University Press, 1965).

31. See the evidence quoted in my book *Human Nature, Election, and History* (Westminster Press, 1977), pp. 78f. and 115f.

32. J. Bohatec, *Calvins Lehre von Staat und Kirche mit besonderer Berücksichtigung des Organismusgedankens* (1937), pp. 147, 154; cf. 125.

33. *Oliver Cromwell: Letters and Speeches,* ed. by Thomas Carlyle, Vol. 5 (repr. New York, 1969), pp. 27f.

34. A paradigm of this is John Locke's celebrated "Essay Concerning the True Original Extent and End of Civil Government," ed. by W. S. Carpenter, in *Two Treatises of Civil Government* (London, [1924], 1962).

35. Reinhold Niebuhr, *The Children of Light and the Children of Darkness: A Vindication of Democracy and a Critique of Its Traditional Defense* (Charles Scribner's Sons, 1945).

36. Thus Hugo Assmann, "Politisches Engagement aus der Sicht des Klassenkampfs," in *Concilium* 9 (1973), pp. 276–282.

37. Gutiérrez, *A Theology of Liberation.* German translation, pp. 41f.

38. John Rawls, *A Theory of Justice* (Harvard University Press, 1971).

39. This problem is too easily dismissed by the so-called dependence theorists, who consider economic dependence as intrinsically evil (but only in cases of dependence on capitalist societies), since they suppose that capitalism itself produces such dependence and underdevelopment. See on this Hans Zwiefelhofer, "Zum Begriff der Dependenz," in *Befreiende Theologie,* ed. by Karl Rahner et al. (Freiburg im Breisgau: Verlag Herder, 1977), pp. 34–45. The essay of Leonardo Boff in the same volume (pp. 46ff., esp. 52f.) illustrates how easily such analyses of economic dependence lend themselves to a diagnosis of "oppression."

40. Manas Buthelezi, "Ansätze Afrikanischer Theologie im Kontext von Kirche in Südafrika," in *Theologie im Konfliktfeld*

Südafrika. Dialog mit Manas Buthelezi, Studien zur Friedensforschung 15, ed. by I. Tödt (Munich and Stuttgart, 1976), pp. 33–132, esp. 43ff. and 50ff.; also 121ff.

41. See esp. James Cone, *God of the Oppressed* (Seabury Press, 1975). For the discussion of Cone's ideas within the circles of "black theology" and for the different emphases in South African as compared to North American black theology, see the informative article of Allan Boesak, "Auszug aus der Wüste. Auf dem Wege in eine Welt der Menschen," in the volume mentioned above (note 40), on pp. 133–159, esp. 137ff., 140ff., 149ff., 155ff.

42. For the distinction between a "relative" and an "absolute" conception of natural law see Troeltsch, *Die Soziallehren der christlichen Kirchen und Gruppen,* pp. 171ff., also 762ff. (E.T. *The Social Teachings of the Christian Churches.*)

43. Dorothee Soelle, *Stellvertretung. Ein Kapitel Theologie nach dem "Tode Gottes"* (1965), p. 176. (E.T. *Christ the Representative: An Essay in Theology After the "Death of God";* Fortress Press, 1967.)

44. Gabriel Vahanian, *The Death of God: The Culture of Our Post-Christian Era* (George Braziller, 1961), p. 187; cf. 175f.

45. Cf. ibid., p. 180.

46. Cf. ibid., p. 177.

47. Thomas J. J. Altizer and William Hamilton, *Radical Theology and the Death of God* (Bobbs-Merrill Co., 1966), p. xii.

48. Ernst Bloch, *Das Prinzip Hoffnung* (Frankfurt, 1959), p. 1493.

49. Ernst Bloch, *Atheismus im Christentum* (Frankfurt, 1969), p. 287. (E.T. *Atheism in Christianity: The Religion of the Exodus and the Kingdom* (Seabury Press, Continuum Books, 1972.)

50. See Peter Berger et al., *The Homeless Mind: Modernization and Consciousness* (Random House, 1973).

51. A direct contribution to psychoanalytical theory is attributed to Buddhist enlightenment by Ashok Kara, "The Ego Dilemma and the Buddhist Experience of Enlightenment," in *Journal of Religion and Health* 18 (1979), pp. 144–157. But he also clearly acknowledges that while "enlightenment is not of the ego" (p. 150), "psychotherapeutic approaches essentially focus on ego existence" (p. 157). That means "they do not attempt to resolve the dread of ego existence," but seek to encourage people "to accept the dread of the arbitrary ground of freedom" (p. 157).

52. See Masao Abe, "Man and Nature in Christianity and Buddhism," *Japanese Religions* 7 (1971), pp. 1–10.

53. Paul Tillich, *Christianity and the Encounter of the World Religions* (Columbia University Press, 1964), pp. 63f.

54. Shin'ichi Hisamatsu, "Atheismus," *Zeitschrift für Missionswissenschaft und Religionswissenschaft* 62 (1978), pp. 268–296.

55. Paul Tillich, *Religionsphilosophie* (1925; Stuttgart, 1962), pp. 61ff. Cf. the discussion in James L. Adams, *Paul Tillich's Philosophy of Culture, Science, and Religion* (Harper & Row, 1965), pp. 52ff.

56. G. Wenz, *Subjekt und Sein. Die Entwicklung der Theologie Paul Tillichs* (Munich, 1979).

57. Abe, "Man and Nature," p. 8.

58. See the explanation of this phrase by Joest, *Ontologie der Person bei Luther,* pp. 233–274.

59. Ibid., pp. 219ff.

60. Abe, "Man and Nature," p. 9. A similar judgment has been expessed by Hisamatsu (see Katsumi Takizawa, lecture cited in note 62, below).

61. Karl Barth, *Kirchliche Dogmatik* I/2, pp. 372ff. (E.T. *Church Dogmatics,* I/2, pp. 340ff.; Edinburgh: T. & T. Clark, 1956.)

62. Katsumi Takizawa, "The Power of the Other and the Power of the Self in Buddhism as Compared to Christianity" (Unpublished lecture, 1977).

63. Masao Abe, "God, Emptiness, and the True Self," in *The Eastern Buddhist* 4 (1969), pp. 15–29; the citation is from p. 20.

64. Abe, "Man and Nature," p. 21.

65. Ibid., p. 22.

66. This question was raised by Tai Dong Han in his article "Mediation Process in Cultural Interaction: A Search for Dialogue Between Christianity and Buddhism." (The place of publication was not identifiable.)